ROBERTSON

MATT AND TOM OLDFIELD

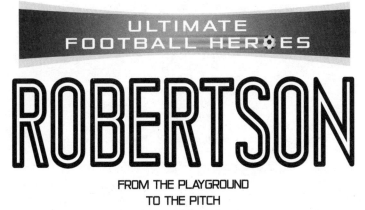

ULTIMATE
FOOTBALL HEROES

ROBERTSON

FROM THE PLAYGROUND
TO THE PITCH

DINO

First published by Dino Books in 2023,
an imprint of Bonnier Books UK,
4th Floor, Victoria House, Bloomsbury Square, London WC1B 4DA
Owned by Bonnier Books,
Sveavägen 56, Stockholm, Sweden

🐦 @UFHbooks
🐦 @footieheroesbks
www.heroesfootball.com
www.bonnierbooks.co.uk

Text © Matt Oldfield 2023
The right of Matt Oldfield to be identified as the author of this work has been
asserted by him in accordance with the Copyright, Designs and Patents Act 1988.

Design by www.envydesign.co.uk

Paperback ISBN: 978 1 78946 492 4
E-book ISBN: 978 1 78946 500 6

British Library cataloguing-in-publication data:
A catalogue record for this book is available from the British Library.

Printed and bound in Great Britain by Clays Ltd, Elcograf S.p.A.

1 3 5 7 9 10 8 6 4 2

For all readers,
young and old(er)

ULTIMATE
FOOTBALL HEROES

Matt Oldfield is a children's author focusing on the wonderful
world of football. His other books include *Unbelievable Football*
(winner of the 2020 Children's Sports Book of the Year) and the
Johnny Ball: Football Genius series. In association with his
writing, Matt also delivers writing workshops in schools.

Cover illustration by Dan Leydon.
To learn more about Dan visit danleydon.com
To purchase his artwork visit etsy.com/shop/footynews
Or just follow him on Twitter @danleydon

TABLE OF CONTENTS

ACKNOWLEDGEMENTS

First of all I'd like to thank everyone at Bonnier Books for supporting me and for running the ever-expanding UFH ship so smoothly. Writing stories for the next generation of football fans is both an honour and a pleasure. Thanks also to my agent, Nick Walters, for helping to keep my dream job going, year after year.

Next up, an extra big cheer for all the teachers, booksellers and librarians who have championed these books, and, of course, for the readers. The success of this series is truly down to you.

Okay, onto friends and family. I wouldn't be writing this series if it wasn't for my brother Tom. I owe him so much and I'm very grateful for his belief in me as an author. I'm also very grateful to the rest of my family, especially Mel, Noah, Nico, and of course Mum and Dad. To my parents, I owe my biggest passions: football and books. They're a real inspiration for everything I do.

Pang, Will, Mills, Doug, Naomi, John, Charlie, Sam, Katy, Ben, Karen, Ana (and anyone else I forgot) – thanks for all the love and laughs, but sorry, no I won't be getting 'a real job' anytime soon!

And finally, I couldn't have done any of this without Iona's encouragement and understanding. Much love to you, and of course to Arlo, the ultimate hero of all. I hope we get to enjoy these books together one day.

CHAPTER 1

AN UNFORGETTABLE NIGHT AT FORMBY HALL

25 June 2020, Liverpool

'Lads, what's the dress code for tonight?' Andy posted on the Liverpool group chat along with a picture. In it, he was wearing not the normal red, but Chelsea blue. It was a shirt that his Scotland teammate, Billy Gilmour, had given him a few months earlier.

Although most of the responses to Andy's photo were pretty rude, it was only a bit of fun. The Liverpool players remained as united as ever. That was one of the key factors in their super-successful 2019–20 season so far – thirty-one games, twenty-eight wins, seventy goals scored and only twenty-one conceded. Along the way, Liverpool had enjoyed easy victories, difficult victories, and fantastic fightbacks, and every player had played their part:

'The Fab Three' up front: Mohamed Salah, Sadio Mané and Roberto Firmino.

The maestros in midfield: Jordan Henderson, James Milner, Fabinho, Gini Wijnaldum.

The superstars in central defence: Virgil van Dijk, Joël Matip, Joe Gomez.

The big guy in goal: Alisson.

And, of course, the flying full-backs: Trent Alexander-Arnold and... Andy! With their amazing energy and incredible crosses, they had assisted twenty goals already.

Together, what a terrific team they made, and now, for one night only, every single one of them was supporting Chelsea. Because if they could beat or draw with Manchester City, then Liverpool's dream would come true and they would be crowned Premier League Champions at last.

The Reds had worked so hard for this and waited so long, through three hard months of lockdown and uncertainty. But now, they were hopefully, finally, just one game away from glory.

'Come On, You Blues!' Andy cheered as the Liverpool squad gathered at Formby Hall to watch the match together. It was going to be a very special night; he just knew it.

First, though, they had a nervous ninety minutes to get through. The Liverpool players sat in rows with their eyes glued towards the big screen, living the match as if they were out there playing themselves.

'Great save!' they cheered when Kepa Arrizabalaga kept out Fernandinho's header.

'Go on, go on… GOOOOOAAAAALLLLL!' they roared as Christian Pulisic raced through to give Chelsea the lead.

'Noooooooooooo!' they groaned when Kevin De Bruyne curled a free kick into the top corner.

With the match tied at 1–1, Andy could hardly bear the tension. Now he knew how his family must feel watching him play every week!

'Phew!' he shouted when Raheem Sterling hit the post for City.

'How did he not score that?' he moaned when Tammy Abraham missed a second tap-in for Chelsea. The TV replays, however, showed that Fernandinho had stopped the shot with his arm.

'HANDBALL! PENALTY!' Andy and his Liverpool teammates yelled loudly as one and continued, 'AND RED CARD!'

They got all three of their wishes, and up stepped Willian to… score from the spot. 2–1 to Chelsea!

'Hendo, you ready to lift that trophy?' Andy teased Jordan, who was sat next to him.

'Don't jinx it, Robbo,' he replied, 'it's not over yet!' But the last fifteen minutes of the match ticked by without a City equaliser, until only seconds were left: 10, 9, 8, 7, 6…

Andy could see the messages flashing up on his phone from his family and friends, but he was too focused on the match to read them.

…5, 4, 3, 2, 1…

When the final whistle blew, Andy jumped out of his seat and ran towards his Liverpool teammates to form a big, happy huddle. They danced and danced all night long, singing that song at last:

Campeones, Campeones, Olé! Olé! Olé!

'We've done it! We've done it!' Andy kept saying
excitedly to everyone he saw, but he still didn't quite
believe the words. In the moment, it was all too
much to take in. It was only a few weeks later that he
was really able to express his emotions properly. He
tweeted:

'Just a kid from Glasgow who had a dream of
playing football. Never did I think winning this was
possible. The best feeling ever and hopefully one of
many more to come #YNWA'

What a fairy tale it was for the fearless Scot! Just
seven years earlier, Andy had been playing amateur
football for Queen's Park in the Scottish Third
Division, after being rejected by his boyhood club
Celtic. But look at what he had achieved since then,
through hard work and his never-give-up attitude.
Unbelievable! The kid from Clarkston was now a
Champions League winner and an English Premier
League champion.

CHAPTER 2

SON OF A CELTIC FAN

After one last quick check to make sure the season tickets were definitely still there in his coat pocket, Brian Robertson turned to his young sons, who were waiting by the front door with restless legs and eager eyes.

'Right, Stephen, Andrew – are you ready to go?' he asked.

'YESSSSSSSSSS!' the two boys cheered together. They'd been ready to go for hours, wearing their green-and-white striped shirts and scarves.

'Okay then – Celtic Park, here we come!'

'HURRRAAAAAAAAYYYYY!'

The boys were bursting with excitement already, but

they still had a long journey ahead of them before they arrived at the football stadium. The Robertsons lived in Clarkston, an area on the southern edge of Glasgow, which was seven miles away from the city centre, and most importantly, from Celtic Park. That was way too far for them to walk, so they would have to travel by car instead, or take a bus or train. All that time sitting still could be really boring, so what could they do to make the journey more entertaining?

'Pop, can you tell us some of your Celtic stories?' Stephen cried out. Although they had heard their dad's tales lots of times before, they still loved listening to them.

'Of course, lad, now which story would you like to hear? The Lisbon Lions?'

Unlike his sons, Brian had grown up in the centre of Glasgow, in an area called Maryhill. Although Partick Thistle's Firhill Stadium was only a short walk away from there, there had only ever been one football club in Brian's life: Celtic. 'The Bhoys', 'The Hoops', 'The Lisbon Lions' of 1967 – how could a little kid not fall in love with that group of local heroes who had gone all the way to lift the European Cup?

On the Wyndford estate, Brian and his friends had grown up kicking a ball around together and dreaming of playing for their favourite team one day. Some of them – including Charlie Nicholas and Jim Duffy – had indeed gone on to become football superstars, but unfortunately not Brian. As a sharp-shooting young striker, he had sadly suffered a bad back injury which meant that he had to wear a metal brace and give up on his professional football dream. So, Brian had put his passion into supporting Celtic instead, and now he had successfully passed that passion on to his children too.

'No, not today, Pop,' Andy decided with a firm shake of his six-year-old head. 'Today, I want to hear about King Kenny!'

Brian's face lit up at the mention of that legendary name. 'Ah yes, King Kenny – good choice, wee man!'

Kenny Dalglish was one of Celtic's greatest ever

players and Brian's ultimate hero. What a footballing wizard! From 1971 to 1977, 'King Kenny' had lit up Celtic Park with his great goals and magic touch, and Brian had been lucky enough to see it happen.

'You know, at first I really hated Liverpool for stealing Kenny away from us like that,' Brian told his sons as they got closer and closer to the stadium, 'but in the end, I grew to love them. I just wanted to watch him play, whoever he was playing for!'

Andy nodded along with understanding. The way Pop felt remembering King Kenny was how he felt about Celtic's latest superstar, Henrik Larsson. He loved everything about the Swedish striker: his long dreadlocks, his excellent shooting, and his cheeky smile whenever he scored.

'Hopefully, Henrik will get another goal today,' Andy thought to himself, as they turned the last corner and there it was looming up in front of them – Celtic Park!

In the background, Andy could see the tops of the stands rising up towards the sky, and in the foreground, the red brick front with the words

'CELTIC FOOTBALL CLUB' written in big, bold letters. Wow, what a beautiful sight! But as a season ticket holder since the age of two, Andy knew that the sights and sounds got even better once they were inside the stadium.

'Come on, let's go in!' he called out impatiently.

When they reached their seats, the chanting had already started, and as the stadium filled up ahead of kick-off, the noise grew louder and louder: 40,000 fans, then 50,000, then 60,000, all singing the same song:

Walk on, walk on,
With hope in your heart,
And you'll never walk alone,
YOU'LL NEVER WALK ALONE!

Wow, what an amazing atmosphere! It gave Andy goosebumps every time, but especially this time, because this was their biggest match of the season so far: the Old Firm Derby against their big local rivals, Rangers, who had won the last two Scottish Premier

League titles.

Come on, Celtic!

With the home crowd cheering them on, the Bhoys pushed forward right from kick-off, full of energy and fight. In the very first minute, the ball bounced down to Larsson in the Rangers box and he passed it through to his strike partner, Chris Sutton, for a simple tap-in. 1–0!

Hurrrraaaaaaaaaaaaaaaaaaaaaaaaaaayyyyyyyyyyyyyyyyyyyy!

The Robertsons bounced up and down in delight, and so did the thousands of other Celtic supporters around them. What a perfect start!

And there was plenty more to come. Stiliyan Petrov soon headed in a second goal, and then Paul Lambert smashed in a third. Celtic were winning 3–0 after only eleven minutes – Andy couldn't believe what he was seeing! Even his dad, who usually shouted and shouted all game long, was lost for words.

Rangers did pull one goal back before half-time, but early in the second half, Andy's hero suddenly came alive again. Collecting the ball from Sutton, Larsson raced away from two defenders, and then coolly chipped a shot over the keeper and into the net. 4–1!

Hurrrraaaaaaaaaaaaaaaaaaaaaaaaaaaayyyyyyyyyyyyyyyyyyyyyy!

As the Celtic celebrations began, Andy turned to Stephen with his mouth wide open in awe. Woah, what a strike – it was by far the greatest goal he'd ever seen!

Twelve minutes later, Larsson scored again, and just before the final whistle, Sutton added another. They had absolutely thrashed their fiercest rivals – 6–2! It was an afternoon that Andy and his brother would never ever forget. As they left Celtic Park, they talked enthusiastically about each of the great goals they'd seen and then argued over the man of the match:

'Sutton was so good today – those Rangers defenders had no idea how to stop him!'

'Yeah, but Larsson scored two as well, and his first one was A-MAZING!'

'Hey boys, you know that could be you two out there playing one day,' Brian said to his sons during that long journey home.

'You really think so, Pop?' Andy replied eagerly. 'Like Uncle Stephen?'

Stephen Frail played for St Johnstone, another club in Scotland's top division, and Andy was desperate to follow in his footsteps. He was already practising his ball skills every day with his brother in the back garden, as well as playing for a local team, Giffnock North, where his dad helped out with the coaching.

'Why not?' Brian shrugged and smiled. 'If you work hard and believe in yourself, anything is possible!'

Andy's eyes grew even wider, as if he'd just seen into the future. An exciting future where his Celtic football dream came true.

CHAPTER 3

FOOTBALL 24/7

That big Celtic dream could wait, though. For now, Andy was just a young boy who wanted to play as much football as possible – anytime, anywhere, and with anyone:

The back garden with his brother,

Hey, Stephen, that's not fair – my shot was definitely going in, wasn't it, Pop?

In the playground at St Joseph's Primary with his schoolmates,

Hurry up, break-time's almost over – next goal wins!

On the pitch at Giffnock Soccer Centre with his club teammates,

Pass it, I'm in space!...Yessssssssssssssss, what a goal!

And in the local park with his friends.

Woah Martin, did you see that? My shooting is getting much better!

Football 24/7 – yes, that was definitely Andy's idea of fun. He loved nothing more than getting out on the grass, or in the street, with a ball at his feet. And if there was no-one else around, he would just work on his passing against a wall on his own – left foot, then right, over and over again...

Playing proper matches was much more fun, though, where he could score lots of great goals and lead his team to victory like Henrik Larsson. Even at a young age, he was determined to win every game.

'Come on, let's keep playing. Five more minutes – we're only one goal behind!'

'But Andy, I'm hungry and I wanna go home for dinner!'

'Food can wait – let's finish this match first!'

Thanks to all those hours spent practising, Andy was starting to really stand out on the pitch. At the age of seven, he went along to a Celtic summer camp where he got to meet one of his heroes, Stiliyan Petrov, and that wasn't even the best bit. No, the best bit was that he played so well that a scout asked to sign him up for the club's community programme. Woah, yessss, his dream was coming true already!

Andy wasn't old enough to join the proper Celtic academy straight away, but after a couple of years in his local district team, at last his first big moment arrived: the trials for the Under-11s! Competing for places against so many other talented young players was a really tough and nerve-wracking experience, but fortunately, there was a very happy ending to the day.

'Mum! Gran!' Andy shouted, bursting into the living room as soon as he got back home with his dad. 'Guess what? I did it, I got in – I'm going to play for Celtic!' In his hand, he proudly held up a special DVD that the coaches had given him, all about the history of the club and 'The Celtic Way'. 'Come on, let's watch it right now!'

Andy couldn't wait to get started. The opportunity to play for the academy every Sunday in the same

green-and-white kit that he watched his heroes wear
at Celtic Park every Saturday? Yes please! This was
his chance to step up and challenge himself against
the top young footballers in the country, and he loved
every minute of it. Although some of the other players
were stronger and more skilful, he didn't let that
bother him. Andy knew that he was in the best place
to learn and develop his skills, with the help of Celtic's
excellent coaches. Plus, he believed in his own ability,
and when it came to football, he was totally fearless.

'Great tackle!'

'Well battled, wee man!'

'Ooof that speed – once you get going, there's no
stopping you, kid!'

The Celtic youth coaches were really impressed by
Andy's never-give-up attitude, and his running, passing
and crossing, but his shooting? Not so much. Oh well,
never mind, he wasn't going to be the next Henrik
Larsson, after all, but if it meant he got to play for
Celtic, he was happy with any position on the pitch,
even left-back!

As he moved through the age groups at the Celtic

academy, Andy's love for football only grew. He wasn't that interested in video games or TV, like a lot of other kids his age; other than a few rounds of golf, all he really wanted to do was play football, and the more matches the merrier. When he wasn't wearing the Celtic shirt, he was wearing the shirt of his secondary school team, and the captain's armband too.

The football coach at St Ninian's High had spotted Andy's special talents straight away. What Joe Fuchs saw was a boy with bursting pace, a lovely left foot, and best of all, a strong character. He was confident, but not arrogant; he was cheeky, but not naughty. Off the pitch, he liked to have a laugh with everyone, but on it, he became a ferocious fighter, who was fully focused on winning. So, when it came to choosing a leader for the school football team, the coach simply had to choose Andy.

'Thanks, Coach – I'm honoured!'

The captain of his school football team and one of Celtic's brightest young stars – Andy really was living the football dream.

CHAPTER 4

SAYING A SAD GOODBYE TO CELTIC

The sports hall at Celtic Park was packed with nervous and excited young players, but the room fell silent as Tommy Burns stepped forward to speak. Back in the 1970s and 1980s, Tommy had been a skilful midfielder, helping Celtic win six Scottish League titles and five Scottish Cups. Now, twenty years later, he spent his time working with the stars of the future as the club's Head of Youth Development.

'Welcome back, boys – we've got another big season ahead of us!' Tommy began with a smile, his voice echoing around the big hall. But really, he wasn't there to laugh and joke; he was there to deliver a serious message to these twelve and thirteen-year-olds. All 120 of them shared the same dream of one day playing for Celtic, but unfortunately, for most of them, that wasn't going to happen. It was Tommy's job to prepare them for the harsh reality of academy football.

'Look, I'll be honest with you,' he told the boys listening, 'if one or two of you make it to the first team, then that's a success and we've done our job.'

Tommy paused to let that bad news sink in. All around the room, heads turned to see how many other players they were up against. Woah, only one or two of them might make it at the club?! So what about all the rest of them?

Sitting in the audience, listening, Andy understood that his Celtic chances were slim, but that didn't stop him believing. Why shouldn't he stay positive and aim for the top? He was doing well at the academy as a central midfielder with a lovely left foot and a never-give-up attitude. Although he was one of the smallest players on his team, he was also one of the toughest tacklers and the hardest workers.

'Well done, Andy – what a challenge, wee man!'

His Under-14s coach, John Gallacher, loved his fearless mindset, and so most importantly, did Mr Burns. Tommy had known Andy for years, and he was a big fan of his, both as a player and a person. Football talent? Tick! Fighting spirit? Tick! Yes, the boy definitely had the potential to make it as a professional footballer, but at a big club like Celtic? They would just have to wait and see.

Andy successfully made it through to Under-15s level, but in May 2008, Tommy tragically died of cancer, at the age of only fifty-one. When he heard the news, Andy was absolutely devastated. Tommy had helped him so much as a coach and as a mentor. What now? The Celtic academy would never be the same again.

Yes, he was right about that. When the club's new Head of Youth Development arrived, he decided to take a very different approach from Tommy's and introduce some big changes. Chris McCart wanted teams full of big, strong physical players, not little, weak-looking guys like Andy. So what if he was fearless in the tackle? It didn't matter. For the

2008–09 season, he was taken out of his usual role in central midfield and moved out to the left wing. Yes, he was left-footed, but…

'Argggh, I haven't got the skills to play this position!' Andy groaned, growing more and more frustrated.

As the end of the year approached, Andy knew that it was make or break time. He watched on anxiously as some of his teammates got full-time contracts, while others had to say goodbye to Celtic. So, what would Andy's fate be? Finally, decision day arrived, and his two coaches called a meeting with him and his parents. Would the news be good or bad? Sadly, Andy was already pretty sure what the answer would be.

'I'm really sorry,' the coaches said, 'but we're releasing you, Andy.'

Noooooooooooooo! Even though it was the news he had been expecting, it was still a crushing blow. After so many years and so much hard work, Andy's Celtic dream was over in an instant. No, unfortunately he wouldn't be one of the lucky one or two who got to play first-team football for the club he had supported all his life, and in that horrible moment, it felt like the end of the world.

Andy managed to hold back the tears in front of his coaches, but once he got home, he cried and cried. Fortunately, he had his family there to help him through his hardest moment.

'I know it hurts right now, but you'll come back even stronger,' his parents comforted him.

'Keep your head up and keep believing,' his Auntie Vera told him, 'because I do. I just know you're going to be a professional footballer one day!'

The next morning, Andy had to get up and go to school, but how was he supposed to tell his friends about what had happened? He felt so embarrassed, and scared to show any weakness. However, as he soon found out, to his friends he had known since nursery, he was still the same old Andy, whether he played for Celtic or not.

'Really sorry to hear that, mate. But I guess the good news is you'll be even fitter for our school games now!'

CHAPTER 5

COMING BACK STRONGER AT QUEEN'S PARK

So, what next? Now that Celtic didn't think he was good enough, was Andy just going to give up on his professional football dream?

No way! He didn't even think about that for a moment. He was still young and he still wanted to give football his all. He wasn't going to let the opinion of one person at one club stop him; there were plenty of other places to play... So Andy took some holiday time away with his family, and then when he returned, he focused on finding a new team.

So, who wanted him? Unfortunately, Andy didn't have as many options as he'd hoped. There was talk that Scottish Premier League clubs Kilmarnock and

Hamilton were interested in signing him, but in the end, neither made a firm offer.

Okay, so what about a team in the First Division instead... or the Second Division? In the end, it was a team in the Third Division who won the race to sign him: Queen's Park. Andy's old Celtic youth coach John Gallacher recommended him, and their coach called him up with a friendly offer:

'Come down and train with us, and see if you like it.'

Sure, why not? Andy agreed straight away. Going from Celtic, one of the biggest clubs in Scotland, to Queen's Park would definitely be a step down, but there were three main things that attracted him to the club:

1) It was local, only a few miles from his family's home in Clarkston,

2) He already knew some other guys from the Celtic academy who were now training there, and

3) The club had a good reputation for developing young players who then moved on to bigger teams.

In recent years, Queen's Park had sold Derek Carcary to Rangers, David Weatherston to St Johnstone, Paul Paton to Partick Thistle, and Steven Saunders to Motherwell. So maybe Andy would be next!

There was one not-so-good thing about signing for Queen's Park, though. It was still an amateur football club, which meant that he wouldn't earn any money. Oh well, that could wait; for now, Andy just wanted to play football, and after enjoying his first few training sessions, he agreed to join the Under-17s.

'Great, welcome to the club!' said David McCallum, the Head of Youth Development, shaking his hand.

Andy's first season, however, was not a very successful one. It took a long time for him to get over his Celtic disappointment, and rediscover his form and never-give-up attitude. Fortunately, the Queen's Park coaches kept believing in him and pushing him to improve.

'Come on, Andy – fight for that ball!'

By the 2010–11 season, Andy was getting back to

his hard-working best, although he was playing in a very different position.

'Left-back?' When his manager first mentioned it, Andy had to repeat it just to make sure he had heard him right. Didn't he mean central midfield?

'No, left-back! Give it a go – we think it's the perfect role for you. We both know you love a tackle, you never stop running, and that left foot can deliver dangerous crosses all day long!'

Hmmm, that did all make sense, and it did sound better than left wing, so Andy did as his coaches asked and gave left-back a go. And the result was... they were right; it was his perfect role! He enjoyed doing all the defensive work, and he loved racing forward from deep on bursting runs.

'Yesssssssss!' Andy called for the ball as he ZOOMED his way up the left wing. Once the pass arrived, he took one touch to control it, then looked up and whipped an incredible cross into the box... GOAL!

'Okay, I think we've found our new left-back!' His manager clapped and cheered.

Although Andy's football career was definitely moving in the right direction again, there was no chance of him getting carried away. He had only just joined the Queen's Park Under-19 Bs, so even playing for the first team in the Scottish Third Division felt like a far-off dream. And as for playing in the Scottish Premier League? Well, that felt like a total fantasy!

Andy was determined to keep playing the game he loved, but soon he would be eighteen, his school days would be over, and he would have a huge decision to make: should he go to college and get a normal job, or continue following his football dream?

CHAPTER 6

ONE MORE YEAR/ FOLLOWING A FOOTBALL DREAM

'One more year' – with a little help from his Auntie Vera, Andy managed to persuade his parents to let him take twelve months away from education, once his time at St Ninian's High School came to an end. He could continue following his football dream at Queen's Park for another season, but after that, if he wasn't progressing, he would have to look at other options. Deal!

'There are lots of things you could do. You could go to college and become a PE teacher,' his mum suggested, 'or go to university and study sports science.'

Sure, anything that involved sport sounded okay!

Andy nodded and promised to think about it, but really, all he wanted to do was play football. One more year – this was his last chance to achieve his dream and he had to make the most of it. He was going to focus on football 24/7, training hard every day to get stronger and work on his weaknesses. But first, he headed off to Greece for a fun, end-of-school holiday with his friends...

One day, as he was partying with his pals, Andy got a phone call from back home. No, it wasn't his family checking up on him; it was the Queen's Park first-team manager, Gardner Speirs.

'Andy, we need you back for pre-season,' he explained. 'We've got games coming up in a few days and Daryll Meggatt's just gone to Alloa Athletic, so we're missing a left-back. Are you up for it?'

Although Andy was having fun in the sun, he could go on holiday anytime. Playing for the Queen's Park first-team, however, was a golden opportunity he couldn't miss. 'Yes, Boss,' he replied eagerly, 'I'm on my way!'

As soon as that call was over, Andy made another

one, this time to his parents: 'Mum, Dad – get me home!'

The first flights were too expensive, but Andy made it back to Glasgow the next day, just in time for the trip to Largs. As the team bus set off, he was buzzing with nervous excitement. This was his big chance to impress the manager and claim that left-back spot, and he was determined to take it.

CRUNCH! Andy fought hard for every ball, showing that he was a lot stronger and fiercer than he looked. Then once Queen's Park had possession...

ZOOM! He raced up the left wing again and again, getting into great positions to...

PING! deliver lots of quality crosses into the box.

'What a ball, Andy!' Speirs clapped and cheered on the sidelines. Wow, this new kid was incredible! His technical ability was clear for all to see, but what really made him special was his never-give-up attitude. Yes, he was exactly the kind of energetic young player that Queen's Park were looking for.

By the end of pre-season, there was no way that Andy was going back to the Under-19s; the first-team squad was where he belonged. Just days later, he was wearing the Number 11 shirt and making his official senior debut for the club in the Scottish Challenge Cup away against Berwick Rangers.

What a feeling! It didn't matter that there were only 372 fans in the crowd watching the match (including his family); Andy was just proud to be playing first-team football, and desperate to put in a strong performance.

'Yesss!' he called for the ball.

In extra-time, with the game tied at 1–1, Andy still had the energy to sprint forward over the halfway line, leaving his tired opponent trailing behind. Approaching the Berwick box, he found himself surrounded by three big defenders, so he calmly slipped a brilliant pass through to his teammate, Owen Ronald. He was about to shoot when a defender fouled him from behind. PENALTY!

Ronald's spot-kick was saved, but the captain, Tony Quinn, was there to score the rebound. 2–1!

'Come onnnnnnnn!' the Queen's Park players cheered in celebration. 'Great work, Andy!'

That wasn't the end, though. Before the final whistle, Berwick fought back to equalise again, sending the match to penalties. Ooooo, the pressure was on – would Andy be brave enough to step up and score? Thankfully Queen's Park won the shoot-out before he had to find out.

Hurrrraaaaaaaaaaaaaayyyyy!

What an unforgettable night! Andy was on his way, and there was no stopping him now. At the age of just eighteen, he started the 2012–13 season as Queen's Park's first choice left-back, playing almost every single minute for 'The Spiders'. Andy knew that he still had lots to work on, though, and so he tried to learn as much as possible from the experienced pros around him in order to keep improving his game:

- ASSISTS!

He set up Jamie Longworth to make it 4–0 away at Elgin City, and then delivered a teasing cross to Tony against Berwick Rangers again.

'Cheers, Andy – what a ball that was!' his captain thanked him.

- GOALS!

He scored one against East Stirlingshire,
and then another against Elgin City.

'Wow, that left foot of yours is lethal!' his manager
congratulated him.

Andy was making a real name for himself and
his timing was perfect. That season, Scottish giants
Rangers were down in the Third Division too,
fighting their way back up after going bankrupt, and
that meant more scouts, more attention, and more
matches live on TV. Amazing – Andy wouldn't get a
better chance to shine!

Unfortunately, Queen's Park lost all four of their
games against Rangers, but even in a 4–0 defeat in
front of 50,000 fans at Ibrox Stadium, their left-back
still looked really dangerous going forward. 'Robertson
really doesn't deserve to be on the losing team today!'
said the commentators on TV.

As much as Andy loved playing for Queen's Park,
there was one thing that he found very frustrating: the
lack of pay.

'Life at this age is rubbish with no money

#needajob,' he tweeted one day.

One of the club's directors, Andrew McGlennan, managed to get him a part-time job at Hampden Park, the national stadium, where first he sold match tickets on the phone and then he worked in the kit room for the Scotland team. But while the extra money was useful, Andy found it all pretty tiring, especially on top of training three times a week and playing matches at the weekends.

The job that he really wanted was professional footballer, and he could feel himself getting closer and closer to his goal. His parents had given him one more year to follow his football dream, and halfway through the season, he already had full-time clubs queuing up to sign him...

CHAPTER 7

LEARNING FROM A CELTIC LEGEND

After making such a strong start, the 2012–13 season ended in disappointment for Queen's Park. They made it through to the promotion play-offs, but there they lost 4–1 to Peterhead. Sadly, The Spiders would be staying in the Third Division, but what about their bright young stars? As he slowly trudged around the pitch, shaking hands with his opponents, Andy already knew that he would be moving on and moving up. But where to?

This time, lots of clubs had shown an interest in him, but in the end, it had been a choice between two Scottish Premier League teams: St Johnstone and Dundee United. Although Dundee United had finished lower in the table that season, Andy decided to sign with them anyway, after meeting their manager, Jackie McNamara.

Andy had grown up watching McNamara play for Celtic as an attacking full-back, so he couldn't wait to work with him as a coach. Plus, McNamara had exciting plans for Dundee United, and young Scottish players were at the heart of it:

Midfielder Stuart Armstrong,

Winger Ryan Gauld,

Centre-back John Souttar,

And now, left-back Andy Robertson!

'I'm not signing you for the future,' McNamara told Andy. 'I'm signing you for the present. You're exactly the kind of quality player I'm looking for to improve my team. I know you've only spent one season in senior football, but if you show me you're ready, I promise you'll get plenty of opportunities here.'

Andy loved the sound of that, but was McNamara just telling him what he wanted to hear?

No – when Andy signed his contract, along with his Queen's Park teammate Aidan Connolly, the Dundee

United manager told the media, 'I will look for both to make an impact as soon as they come in.' And when Andy arrived for his first day of training and thought he might be starting with the Under-20s, McNamara showed him straight into the first-team dressing room.

Wow, okay – his new manager really did believe in him! Now, Andy had to believe in himself and show his new teammates what he could do...

When Dundee United's new left-back walked into the dressing room for the first time, the club captain, John Rankin, saw a skinny schoolkid and thought, 'Really?' But when he watched Andy play in a pre-season friendly against German club Union Berlin, he soon changed his mind.

CRUNCH!

'Woah, he's tougher than he looks!'

ZOOM!

'Wow, this kid never stops running!'

PING!

'And he can cross the ball too – okay, we've got a seriously good player here!'

Dundee United had given Andy a two-year contract:

one to settle in, and then the second to push for a place in the starting line-up. But why wait? He was already feeling confident, and the club had just lost their first choice left-back: Barry Douglas. Perfect – a starting spot was up for grabs! Andy was determined to fill the gap straight away, just like he had done at Queen's Park.

So, what could he do to impress his new manager? The main thing was to listen and learn from the former Celtic legend. At training, McNamara often did special full-back drills with Andy and the Dundee United right-backs, Keith Watson and Mark Wilson, focusing on thing like:

Where to pass when under pressure,

When to stay back and when to push forward,

How to stop crosses from coming into the box,

How to deal with crosses if they did come in…

'Top work, Robbo!' his manager praised him after heading the ball far away from danger.

Andy did a decent job in Dundee United's first three league games of the season, but it was in the fourth game against St Johnstone, the club he had nearly signed for, where everything really clicked. With his team already winning 2–0, Andy got the ball and raced forward with it. After spinning away from one tackle, he split the St Johnstone defence with a sensational through-ball for Gary Mackay-Steven… GOAL – 3–0!

As the home crowd at Tannadice Park went wild, Gary gave Andy a thank you high-five, while on the touchline, McNamara clapped and smiled.

'That's more like it, lads – keep it up!'

With his first assist and the support of his teammates, Andy now had the confidence to make more attacking runs. 'Don't worry, I can cover you,' John, his captain, told him.

Perfect! Against Motherwell, Andy collected the ball just outside his own box and ZOOM! off he raced, over the halfway line and towards the opposition penalty area. No-one came across to close him down, so in the end, he decided to shoot. BANG! He fired the ball past the keeper and into the bottom corner.

Gooooooooooooooooooooaaaaaaaaaaaaaaaaalllllllllllllllllll llllllllll!!!!!!!!!!!!!!!!!!!!!

'Yesssssssssssss!' Andy yelled with passion as he bounced up and down in front of the Dundee United supporters. What a way to score his first goal for the club, and his first goal in the Scottish Premier League!

After fewer than ten games at Dundee United, Andy was on fire at the top level already, and he was feeling totally fearless now. A few weeks later, away at Motherwell, United were 3–0 up, with less than five minutes to go. It looked like game over, but strange things had happened to them at Fir Park before.

'Just stay back and keep things tight until the end,' John told his left-back.

Andy nodded, but moments later as Dundee United attacked, he decided to disobey his captain. He had already hit the bar earlier in the game, and now he wanted one last chance to score. So when John got the ball and looked to his left, there was Andy, all the way forward on the edge of the Motherwell box.

'Robbo, what did I just tell you?!' John muttered angrily, but he still passed to him.

BANG! Andy fired a first-time shot into the top corner. 4–0!

51

Gooooooooooooooooooooaaaaaaaaaaaaaaaalllllllllllllllllll
lllllllll!!!!!!!!!!!!!!!!!!!!!

There was no arguing with a super-strike like that.
'Fine, Robbo – you win this time!' John shouted as he
ran over to celebrate with him.

CHAPTER 8

GREAT DAYS AT DUNDEE UNITED/FLATMATES HAVING FUN

What a flying start! Instead of a whole year, it had only taken Andy a few weeks to settle into his new life at Dundee United. With his cheeky smile and impressive performances, he had quickly become a key part of the squad, earning the respect of senior pros like John, and making close friends with the team's other more junior players.

'Nice one, Robbo – you're one of us now!'

Andy got on so well with three of his young teammates that he even ended up sharing a flat with them. Goalkeeper Joe McGovern, defender John Souttar, and attacker Ryan Gauld all shared the same dream of one day playing for their country, and they shared the same interests too – football, football, and football! When they weren't at training or playing matches, they were usually outside somewhere having a kickaround together. Sometimes, it was just a bit of two-touch passing on the garden patio, but if the sun was out and they were feeling fresh, they couldn't help themselves…

'It's a good thing the Boss can't see us now!' Joe joked as they were returning home from playing a tiring match in the park. 'Hey Gauldy, what's for dinner?'

Ryan shook his head. 'No way, mate – I'm not cooking! Why don't you do it?'

It was Joe's turn to shake his head. 'John? Robbo?'

Andy broke the silence with a laugh. 'I guess we'll be having another takeaway then!'

Yes, Dundee United's whizz-kids were having lots of fun together, both on and off the Scottish Premier League pitches. Against Partick Thistle, John calmly dribbled the ball out of defence and then played it forward to Stuart, who flicked it on to Ryan. After a neat first touch, he slid a perfect pass across to the left wing, for his friend to race on to…

ZOOM! Andy was already on the run, sprinting into the space, and so the Partick players had no chance of catching him. He reached the ball first and dribbled into the box, before firing a fierce shot into the bottom corner.

Goooooooooooooooooooaaaaaaaaaaaaaaaaalllllllllllllllll lllllllllll!!!!!!!!!!!!!!!!!!!!!

Two goals in two games: Dundee United's left-back was looking lethal! Andy had finished off another fantastic team move, and as he stood there pumping his fists in front of the fans, Ryan joined him, jumping up for a piggy-back.

'Come onnnnnnnnnnnnn!' Robbo and Gauldy cried out together with glee.

Their futures looked very bright, but how far could each of them go? People were already calling Ryan 'Baby Messi' and he was being linked with big clubs like Liverpool, Real Madrid and Manchester United. Suddenly, there were lots of top scouts there in the stadium watching every time Dundee United played, and Ryan wasn't the only promising youngster who caught their attention.

'I really like the look of that left-back. He's got great energy going forward and he doesn't mind doing the dirty work in defence.'

'Yeah, and he can cross the ball beautifully too. I'll be talking to the boss about him, for sure.'

Wow – less than a year earlier, Andy had been playing for Queen's Park in the Scottish Third Division, and now he had huge English Premier League clubs like Everton wanting to sign him! He wasn't getting carried away, though. How could he, when he still had to clean the boots of the senior players, even though he was now starring for the first team?

'Urgh, these ones are stinking!'

But despite that dull and sometimes disgusting task, Andy was still loving life at Dundee United. There was no way he was ready to move on yet, and leave Scotland behind. He really enjoyed being part of such a talented young team who played exciting, flowing football and were getting better and better all the time. By March 2014, they were up to fourth in the league and through to the Scottish Cup semi-finals.

There, Dundee United faced a club that Andy knew very well from his days in the Third Division and also from his years supporting Celtic: Rangers! At Queen's Park, he had lost all four games against them; now, he wanted revenge.

'Come on, we can win this!' John, their captain clapped and cheered in the changing room before they walked out onto the pitch in front of 40,000 fans at Ibrox.

Although Rangers were still down in the Second Division, they were battling their way back to the top, and reaching the Scottish Cup final would be the perfect way to show it. Dundee United, however, were determined to stop them.

Early in the first half, Rangers won a corner and their captain, Lee McCulloch, headed the ball goalwards, but Andy stood tall in his own six-yard box and blocked it. Then, as the rebound dropped to another Rangers player, he bravely threw his body in front of the shot and deflected it away from danger.

'Yessss, let's goooooo!' Andy cried out, slapping his

legs with passion.

After that amazing piece of defending, Dundee United came alive and pushed forward on the attack. Andy's scuffed shot flew straight at the keeper, but Stuart found the bottom corner, and then so did Gary Mackay-Steven. 2–0! Although Rangers pulled a goal back before half-time, Dundee United stayed strong and then scored a late third goal to secure the victory. Yes, they were through to the Scottish Cup Final!

When the final whistle blew, Andy, Ryan and John all rushed towards each other with huge grins on their faces, just three flatmates having fun together. What a feeling! There were no big celebrations yet, though; those could wait. Dundee United didn't just want to be in the final; they wanted to win it.

That was the main thing on Andy's mind, even when he beat Ryan and Stuart to win Scotland's Young Player of the Year award. Wow, what a wonderful year he was having, but as ever, Andy was thinking about his team, not himself. 'If we could win the Scottish Cup that would top off the most amazing season,' he said in his winner's speech.

In the final, they faced St Johnstone, the club Andy had almost signed for a year earlier. Dundee United had finished two places above them in the league, but could they now beat them in the biggest game of all?

In the first half, Andy raced up the left wing and curled a beautiful cross into the box for Ryan Dow to flick on. The ball flew past the diving keeper and towards the bottom corner, but no, it bounced off the post instead. Andy threw his hands to his head in disbelief – what bad luck!

Unfortunately for Dundee United, the bad luck continued. Nadir Çiftçi's free kick hit the crossbar, Andy's shot was saved, and Stuart's shot was blocked. At the other end, meanwhile, St Johnstone scored twice from goalkeeping mistakes.

'Noooooo!' Andy groaned, letting his shoulders slump, as the second goal went in. It was game over. After so much excitement, Dundee United's cup final had ended in bitter disappointment.

But once his anger and frustration began to fade, Andy was able to look back happily at an amazing, life-changing season:

    44 games,

    5 goals,

    6 assists,

    1 Scotland Young Player of the Year award,

    1 Scottish Cup runner's up medal,

And most amazing of all,

    His first cap for his country.

CHAPTER 9

SCOTLAND'S NEW/RISING STAR

It had all happened so fast. In October 2013, Andy joined the Scotland Under-21s for the first time, and the following month, he was training with the senior squad. All of a sudden he was sharing a pitch with Premier League stars like Alan Hutton and Robert Snodgrass!

Andy tried not to think too much about it, and just enjoy the experience. It was a golden opportunity to learn from these top players, and he was determined to make the most of it. Plus, it was also a great chance to impress the national team manager, Gordon Strachan. Although Andy was still only nineteen years old, left-back was a problem position for Scotland,

and hopefully he could be the one to solve it. So throughout each and every session, he focused on doing what he did best:

CRUNCH! fighting hard for every ball,

ZOOM! racing up the left wing again and again, and getting into great positions for...

PING! delivering lots of quality crosses into the box.

And his plan worked. At a press conference afterwards, Strachan mentioned two players who he thought had performed particularly well at the camp:

Midfielder James Morrison...

And Andy!

Amazing – mission accomplished! A week later, Andy was back with the Under-21s, but at least the senior manager now knew who he was and what he could do.

And Strachan didn't forget. Another four months passed before he named his next Scotland squad, but when he did, there was a new name amongst the list of defenders:

ANDREW ROBERTSON.

Really, a senior Scotland international? Wow, what

unbelievable news and what an honour! It was the
new proudest moment of Andy's football career
so far. As a young boy, he had always dreamed of
representing his country, but after saying goodbye to
Celtic at the age of fifteen, he had thought that would
never happen. A few incredible years later, however,
his dream was about to come true.

'Mum, Dad, guess what?' Andy announced with
great excitement. 'I've been called up to play for
Scotland!'

'Yessssssss, son!'

'CONGRATULATIONS!'

In amongst all the joy, however, there was a
touch of sadness because one of Andy's other biggest
supporters wouldn't be there to see him wear the
navy blue shirt for the first time. His Auntie Vera,
who had never stopped believing and cheering him
on, from Celtic to Dundee United, had tragically died
just a few months earlier. She had always been a very
passionate Scot, so he knew that this moment would
mean so much to her.

Andy was determined to do his auntie proud, but

would he get a chance to play this time? Scotland only had one match – a friendly, away against Poland – and as one of the youngest in a big squad, he wasn't expecting any game-time. Just getting to sit on the subs bench was a great experience.

After sixty minutes, however, the score was still 0–0 and so the Scotland coaches told two of the subs to start warming up:

Phil Bardsley,

...and Andy!

He tried not to get his hopes up as he jogged and stretched along the side of the pitch, but when he returned to the bench, Strachan pointed and called him over.

'Me?' Andy checked, and his manager nodded. Hurray, he was coming on to make his senior Scotland debut! As he removed his team tracksuit to reveal his Number 13 shirt, he tried to take lots of long, deep breaths to slow his racing heartbeat. It was a massive moment, in front of friends and family, and he was desperate to shine for his country.

'Just go out there and play your own game,'

Strachan told Andy who was waiting on the touchline. 'If you make mistakes, no problem; but don't be scared to try. Do what you do at Dundee United, and you'll be great.'

'Yes, Boss.' Andy nodded and smiled. Show no fear; yes, he could definitely do that. His manager's message was still in his head when at last the ball came to him. So, after taking his first touch in international football, ZOOM! Andy burst forward at speed, up over the halfway line, before passing to a teammate.

Although his run didn't lead to a goal, it was exactly the kind of positive football that Strachan wanted his Scotland side to play. 'Andy came on there and the first time he picked it up he drove about thirty yards,' he praised him afterwards. 'I thought, "That's fantastic".'

When he heard his manager's words, Andy felt on top of the world. What a start to his international career! After playing those twenty-five minutes against Poland, however, he was hungry for more. Strachan started Andy in their next match, a 2–2 draw against Nigeria, and then he got to play the full ninety minutes against Georgia and Ireland. And what was the result in both? A 1–0 win for Scotland!

There was no doubt that Andy was his country's best left-back now, and up next was their biggest game of all – Scotland vs England. And to make things extra special for him, the match would be played at Celtic Park, the home of all of Andy's football dreams.

'Come on, we haven't beaten them since the days of Dalglish!' he reminded his teammates before kick-off.

Unfortunately the game ended in a 3–1 win for England, but Andy was at the centre of everything good for Scotland.

In the first half, he raced onto Steven Naismith's pass and delivered a dangerous ball that bounced and skidded across the box. Unfortunately, however, Scott Brown couldn't quite reach it with his outstretched leg.

Noooooooooooooooooooooooooooooooo!

Then late in the second half, with Scotland losing 2–0, Andy got the ball on the left and pushed forward

on a brilliant attack. After dribbling past Raheem
Sterling, he poked a pass through to Johnny Russell,
and then carried on running for the one-two. When
the ball came back to him on the edge of the six-yard
box, Andy kept calm and scored.

Yessssssssssssssssssssssssssssssssssssssssss!

Goooooooooooooooooooaaaaaaaaaaaaaaaalllllllllllllllllllll
llllllllll!!!!!!!!!!!!!!!!!!!!!

What a moment – Andy had scored his first goal
for Scotland, against England, and at Celtic Park!
After high-fiving Johnny, he raced back for the restart,
raising both arms to the sky for Auntie Vera along
the way. But while that goal made him a hero in
his homeland, it didn't go down so well in his new
adopted country…

CHAPTER 10

ENGLAND
CALLING

At the end of Dundee United's 2013–14 season, Andy
had a big decision to make. Should he stay or should
he go? In Scotland, there was only one bigger club
that he could move to, and that was Celtic, who:

a) Already had a talented left-back, Emilio Izaguirre,
and

b) Had already released him at the age of fifteen.

Okay, so what other options did Andy have? Well,
there were lots of teams in England trying to sign him,
but was he ready to leave Scotland yet? He certainly
didn't feel ready to move away from his friends and
family, but when the Hull City manager Steve Bruce
invited him down for a meeting, Andy agreed. Why

not? It was worth a look.

Hull were heading into their second season in the Premier League, and so Bruce was looking to strengthen his squad. The club had already signed midfielder Jake Livermore from Tottenham and Andy's Scotland teammate Robert Snodgrass from Norwich City, but they were looking to add youth as well as experience, and that's why they wanted Andy.

It had only taken Hull's Head of Recruitment, Stan Ternent, two trips to Scotland to make up his mind about him. On that first trip, however, he had actually gone to Dundee United vs Kilmarnock to scout one of Andy's teammates, Stuart Armstrong. That day, Stuart grabbed a goal and an assist, but he still wasn't the stand-out star, according to Ternent. That was Dundee United's speedy little left-back, who spent the whole match bombing up and down the wing, delivering top-quality crosses.

'So, what did you think?' Bruce asked Ternent the next day on the phone.

'The one we looked at is not for us,' he replied, 'but I can't believe who else I saw...'

To make sure that Andy's masterclass wasn't a one-off, Ternent did go back to watch one more Dundee United match, but at half-time, he closed his notebook and went home. He had seen enough. On the way, he called Bruce with a clear message:

'We have to sign this Robertson kid, 100 per cent.'

And after watching Andy play himself, Bruce agreed. With his positive attitude and energy, the boy was perfect for the high-speed, end-to-end football of the Premier League. Now, for the hard part: the Hull manager needed to persuade the young left-back to leave Scotland and come to England.

Fortunately, one long, friendly chat was all it took to change Andy's mind. From the very beginning, Bruce was full of positivity, and he made it very clear that he wasn't signing him as a player for the future. No, instead of sitting on the bench, the manager saw him as a regular starter. 'I've seen what I need to see,' he explained. 'You're ready for this!'

Really? Okay! If he was being honest, Andy still found the idea of playing in the English Premier League a bit scary, but his ambition was to challenge himself at the highest level one day. So why not now? What if he never got another chance? If the Hull manager believed in him, then he would make that massive step-up and give it his best shot.

'Let's do it!' Andy told his agent.

The deal was done on 29 July 2014, the same day that another talented young defender, Harry Maguire, signed from Sheffield United. Posing for photos in Hull shirts together, holding orange-and-black scarves above their heads, Andy and Harry hit it off straight away. They were the same age and they also had similar stories of working their way up from the lower leagues.

'And now look where we are,' Harry said with a huge grin on his face, 'about to play in the Premier League!'

Andy couldn't wait, but first, he had some settling in to do at Hull. He was walking into a very strong squad, featuring top players he had grown up watching on TV, like Michael Dawson and Tom Huddlestone. Could he really compete with them? Fortunately, as well as Harry, he also had two Scottish teammates, Robert Snodgrass and Allan McGregor, who helped him feel at home.

'Don't worry, Robbo,' Robert and Allan joked, 'you can still buy Irn-Bru down here!'

Andy had already missed most of Hull's pre-season matches, so he had some catching up to do. What could he do to impress his new manager and show him that he was ready to be a regular starter?

ZOOM! At the end of each training session, he did extra 100m sprints on his own to increase his super-speed...

PING! He practised curling lots of dangerous left-foot crosses into the box...

And

BANG! He scored in Hull's last pre-season match against VfB Stuttgart.

Instead of left-back, Bruce asked Andy to play on the left of the midfield that day. Brilliant! It meant a little less defending, and a lot more attacking...

In the twelfth minute, striker Nikica Jelavić's shot was saved by the keeper, but as the ball ran loose, there was Andy, racing in at the back post, to poke it in and score on his Hull debut.

Goooooooooooooooooooaaaaaaaaaaaaaaaaallllllllllllllllllll
llllllllll!!!!!!!!!!!!!!!!!!!!!

'Yessssss, Robbo!' his teammates congratulated him
as they all celebrated together.

So, had Andy done enough to earn a starting spot
for Hull's first Premier League game against QPR?
Not yet, but luck was on his side. The day before
the match, his main rival for the left-back role, Liam
Rosenior, picked up an injury in training. There was
only one thing for it:

'Andy, you're in!' Bruce told him three hours before
kick-off. 'Go out there and do what you can do.'

'Yes, Boss!'

Woah – Andy hardly had time to think, let alone tell
his family, who were all travelling down to London
for the match. They were expecting him to be on the
bench, but now, they would get to see him starting
instead!

So, could Andy take his big chance, just like he'd
done at Queen's Park and Dundee United? Yes! As
usual, he showed no fear on the football pitch. Early

on, he raced up the left wing and set up Nikica with an excellent cross, but sadly the striker couldn't quite score. Then later in the game, with his team winning 1–0, Andy cleared a QPR header off his own goal line. Hurray, not only was he a Premier League player now, but he was already also a Hull City hero!

CHAPTER 11

PAINFUL LESSONS IN THE PREMIER LEAGUE

Unfortunately, after that first victory away at QPR, Hull only won one of their next sixteen games. Frustrating draws and disappointing defeats – for Andy, life in the Premier League was turning out to be a real learning experience. Week after week, he was defending against some of the best wingers in the world:

Manchester City's David Silva,

Arsenal's Alexis Sánchez,

Manchester United's Ángel Di María,

Chelsea's Eden Hazard…

At times, trying to stop them felt like mission impossible, but Andy always managed to stay positive, no matter what. Even when he made a bad mistake

which allowed Newcastle United to score a late
equaliser, he didn't let his head drop too much. He was
still young and new to the Premier League, so there
was plenty of room for improvement.

After each match, Andy asked himself the same
question: 'What can I do to become a better player?'
At the training ground every day, he practised his
positioning, his heading, and his one-vs-one defending,
and he spent time building up his upper-body strength
too.

'That's it – add some muscle to those skinny arms of
yours!' Robert Snodgrass teased him in the gym.

As well as working hard on his weaknesses, Andy
also kept doing what he did best at Dundee United.
Against Manchester City, he got the ball and ZOOM!
he raced forward with it, up the left wing, leaving
James Milner trailing behind. As he approached the
penalty area, he looked up and saw Nikica making a
run in the middle. Andy's clever cross almost reached
him, but Vincent Kompany stretched out a leg and
cleared it away.

'Great idea, Robbo!' Bruce clapped and cheered.

'We need more of that!'

Yes, Boss! So, a week later against Crystal Palace, Andy raced up the left wing again, and this time, he whipped in a high-quality cross for Mohamed Diamé to head home. 1–0!

'That's more like it!' Andy thought to himself as the Hull team celebrated together. Although Mohamed got the goal and the glory, Andy got lots of hugs and high-fives for his assist, as well as lots of praise from his manager after the final whistle.

'I have to be honest and say that Andy has totally and utterly shocked me with his ability to step in,' Bruce said. 'For a twenty-year-old to play at the highest level – he's going to have a big, big future.'

Thanks, Boss! But just as he was finding his best form in the Premier League, Andy's season turned sour. Against Everton, he suffered an ankle injury that kept him out of action for the whole of January. Noooooooo! He had to watch helplessly from the stands as his team struggled without him.

West Brom 1 Hull City 0,
West Ham 3 Hull City 0…

By the time Andy was finally back to full fitness, Hull were in a serious relegation fight. So, to make his team harder to beat, Bruce switched to a more defensive 3-5-2 formation and found someone more experienced to replace Andy. With Robbie Brady doing really well in the left wing-back role, Andy had to watch sadly from the subs bench – Hull beat Aston Villa and QPR without him.

'Am I ever going to get my place back?' he wondered miserably.

The answer was: 'yes and no'. For the rest of the season, Andy moved in and out of the starting line-up as The Tigers climbed out of the relegation zone, but then slipped back into trouble. Uh-oh, were they going down?

Despite his best efforts, Andy couldn't help stop the slide. Against Chelsea, he dribbled his way past two defenders and delivered a perfect cross for Ahmed Elmohamady to score. But after conceding another late goal, Hull lost the match 3–2.

'Not again!' Andy groaned, and the bad news continued. Unfortunately, that turned out to be his last start of the season. He missed the whole month of April due to another ankle problem, and in the final weeks, Bruce only brought him on when matches already seemed lost:

Hull City 1 Arsenal 3,

Tottenham 2 Hull City 0...

Uh-oh, with one game to go, Hull were down in eighteenth place, two points behind the nearest team, Newcastle United. So, who was their last, must-win match against? The mighty Manchester United!

Come on, you Tigers!

The atmosphere was electric at the KC Stadium (now called the MKM Stadium), but even when United had a player sent off, Hull still couldn't find a way to score. Andy came on for the last ten minutes, but it was too little too late. The match ended 0–0, which meant Hull were relegated.

Nooooooooooooooo!

After the final whistle, Andy stood there on the pitch for ages with his hands on his hips, staring down at the grass below his feet. It was a horrible moment, one of the worst of his football career. The team had fought hard all year, but ultimately, they had failed, and he felt like he had let the fans down. Now, there was only one way to make things better: by helping Hull to win promotion back to the Premier League next season.

CHAPTER 12

BOUNCING
BACK UP!

That summer, 2015, Andy was linked with a big-money move to Aston Villa, but when the Hull squad met up for pre-season in July, he was still there and raring to go.

'Obviously, we had a disappointing end to last season,' he told Tigers TV during the club's training camp in Portugal, 'and we're looking to put that right. The only way is to get back to the big league.'

Winning promotion to the Premier League, however, wasn't going to be easy. In the Championship, Hull would have to play a lot of matches, against a lot of very good teams: Middlesbrough, Burnley, QPR, Derby County,

Sheffield Wednesday… The list went on and on.

Challenge accepted! Andy couldn't wait to get started. Although Hull had lost a few important players, like Nikica and Robbie, the core of the team was still the same:

Allan in goal,

Curtis Davies and Michael Dawson in defence,

Mohamed, Ahmed and Tom Huddlestone in midfield,

And Abel Hernández in attack.

That was good because the boys who had experienced the pain of relegation were really determined to bounce back up.

Against Fulham, Tom played the corner back to Andy, who curled in a beautiful cross, right onto Ahmed's head. 1–0!

Against Birmingham City, Andy got the ball in his own half, burst past three defenders, and dribbled all the way into the opposition penalty area. There, he slid a pass across to Abel, who fired into the bottom corner. 2–0!

'What brilliant work from Andy Robertson!' the TV

commentators exclaimed.

While he had learned a lot during his first year in the Premier League, Andy found he was learning even more in his second in the Championship. With the team playing two matches almost every week, his fitness improved, and so did his defending and his attacking.

Away at Brentford, his amazing form continued. As soon as he played the ball to Sam Clucas, ZOOM! Andy was off, sprinting forward for the one-two. What a run! When the return pass arrived, he was into the box, with his just the keeper to beat...

Goooooooooooooooooooaaaaaaaaaaaaaaaalllllllllllllllllll llllllllll!!!!!!!!!!!!!!!!!!!

'Yesssssssss!' Andy yelled, pumping his fists in front of the fans. His first official goal for Hull!

So far, the season was going perfectly according to plan. With fifteen games played, The Tigers were top of the Championship table!

The Championship was a long and challenging competition, however, and unfortunately, Hull couldn't hold on to first place. After a poor run of results in March, they slipped down to second, then third, then fourth... Uh-oh, if they weren't careful, they wouldn't even qualify for the play-offs!

There was no way Andy was going to let that happen, though. With Hull drawing 1–1 away at Reading, Tom suddenly switched the ball from the crowded right wing to the spacious left. Danger alert! With his first touch, Andy darted away from his marker, and then he dribbled forward towards the penalty area.

'SHOOT!' the Hull supporters urged.

So, as the Reading defenders closed in, Andy pulled his left leg back and BANG! His shot was low, hard and very accurate, sending the ball fizzing into the bottom corner. 2–1!

Goooooooooooooooooooaaaaaaaaaaaaaaaalllllllllllllllllll llllllllll!!!!!!!!!!!!!!!!!!!!

Andy stood there in front of the fans with his left fist in the air, as his teammates raced over to hug their hero.

'Yesss, Robbo – what a run!'

Thanks to Andy's wonderful winning goal, Hull stayed fourth in the table, and two weeks later, he got his fifth assist of the season in a 2–0 victory over Brentford. Hurray, their play-off place was secured! Now, if they played well, the Tigers were just three games away from bouncing back up to the Premier League.

First up: Derby County away. At a packed Pride Park Stadium, Hull defended well under pressure, and took their chances on the attack.

First, Jake Livermore pounced on a poor pass and set up Abel to score his twenty-second goal of the season. 1–0!

Then just before half-time, Moses Odubajo's shot deflected off a Derby defender and into the net. 2–0!

That was already a good lead to take home for the second leg, but Hull wanted more. In the last seconds, they cleared a Derby corner and raced forward on the counterattack. Sam flicked the ball on to Jake, who played it through to Moses. As two defenders surrounded him, he slid it left to Andy, who thought about passing but decided to shoot from distance instead. BANG! Although he slipped as he kicked it, his left-foot strike was still as accurate as ever. 3–0!

Goooooooooooooooooooooaaaaaaaaaaaaaaaaallllllllllllllllll
lllllllllll!!!!!!!!!!!!!!!!!!!!!

After watching the ball roll into the bottom corner,
Andy jumped up and threw both arms in the air.
'Come onnnnnn!' he cried out, bouncing his way
over to the bench to celebrate with Mohamed and the
other subs. It felt like a massive moment for Hull –
surely, they couldn't lose the semi-final now?

But Derby didn't give up and by half-time in
the second leg, The Tigers were in trouble. Andy's
Scotland teammate Johnny Russell scored the first,
and Andy himself scored the second, mis-kicking the
ball into his own net.

Noooooooooooooooo! 3–2 – what was going on?
Thankfully, after a big team-talk from Bruce, Hull
came back out and played a lot better in the second
half. Derby tried and tried to grab an equalising goal,
but Andy and his fellow defenders stood strong and
stopped them again and again. At last, it was all over,
and they were through to the play-off final. As their
happy supporters stormed the pitch, Andy breathed a
big sigh of relief. Phew!

Hull were expecting to meet Brighton and Hove Albion in the final, but instead, they faced Sheffield Wednesday. They had drawn twice in the league that season, so which team would win the '£170-million match' in front of 70,000 fans at Wembley?

After a long, anxious build-up, the clock finally struck 5pm – time for kick-off! Once he was out on the pitch, Andy found that his nerves disappeared. Suddenly, it was just another football match that he was determined to win.

'Let's goooooooooooooo!'

With the pressure on, it turned out to be a very tense game, but the Tigers were the team on top. In the first half, Tom, Michael and Abel all missed great chances to score, while Mohamed hit the post. So close!

'Keep going!' Bruce clapped and cheered on the sidelines. 'The goal will come!'

Early in the second half, another golden opportunity arrived – this time for Andy. On a quick counterattack, Moses slid the ball across the box, past the last defender, and onto the left-back's left boot. Perfect! Andy actually had time and space to take a touch, but instead, he panicked and shot straight away, slicing the ball high over the bar.

Noooooooooooooooo! Andy buried his face in his hands; he couldn't believe it. What a chance to be Hull's Wembley hero, and he had wasted it! Luckily for him, however, fifteen minutes later, Mohamed scored with a sensational long-range strike. 1–0!

Yessssssssssssssssss! Andy raced over to celebrate with his teammates in front of their wildly cheering fans, but he knew that the job wasn't done yet. They had twenty minutes of defending to do first:

BLOCK!

HEADER!

TACKLE!

INTERCEPTION!

CLEARANCE!

The Hull players worked so hard together until at last, the final whistle blew. Hurraaaaaaaaay, they had done it; they had achieved their aim of bouncing back up to the Premier League!

With a huge smile on his face, Andy ran around the pitch, hugging every teammate and coach he could find. Promoted as play-off winners – what a way to end the season! And already he couldn't wait for the next one to begin.

CHAPTER 13

MORE PREMIER LEAGUE PAIN

Andy was really hoping that his second spell in the Premier League would be more successful, but unfortunately, things got off to a difficult start. Mohamed decided to move on to Newcastle, and midway through pre-season training, Hull's manager announced that he was leaving the club.

Nooooo! Why? It was really sad news for Andy, who had loved working with Steve Bruce. He had taught him so much and he would always be grateful to him for giving him a chance to shine at the highest level.

So, who would take over now? The answer, at least to start with, was their old assistant manager, Mike

Phelan, but for how long, no-one seemed to know.

Despite the off-field problems, Hull started the new season with two hard-fought wins over Leicester City and Swansea City, and so for a few days, they sat joint top of the Premier League table! The good times didn't last long, though. The Tigers didn't win a single game in September, or in October, and eventually they slipped down into the relegation zone.

'Not again!' Andy did his best to stay positive, but it wasn't easy when Hull kept losing week after week. The team spirit and confidence that they had shown in the Championship had totally disappeared, and in January, things got even worse when the club decided to sell some of their best players. Jake Livermore joined West Brom, Robert Snodgrass went to West Ham – and as for Andy? Burnley tried to sign him, but the offer was rejected, and so he stayed to battle on for the rest of the season.

Come on, you Tigers!

When Hull fell to the bottom of the Premier League, the chairman decided to try another new manager, Marco Silva. The Portuguese coach was young and full of fresh ideas, and at first, he got the team playing exciting, winning football again. From 1–0 down, Hull fought back to beat Bournemouth 3–1, and it all started with one of Andy's top-quality curling crosses, which Abel Hernández attacked with pace and power.

'Yesssssss, that's more like it!' Andy cheered.

He was enjoying his first experience of working with a foreign manager, and the team's hard work on the training pitch was already paying off. Under Silva, the Tigers were looking fitter, tougher and a lot more organised. Away at Old Trafford, Andy and his fellow defenders did a brilliant job of keeping all of Manchester United's amazing attackers quiet. A 0–0 draw gave them another precious point. Maybe Hull could still stay up, after all!

Their problem, however, was performing that well consistently. After a surprise win against Liverpool, they then drew with Burnley and lost to Leicester City and Everton.

'We're going down!' their frustrated fans chanted at the full-time whistle.

The situation really didn't look good, but Andy refused to give up and get relegated again without a fight. In April, he helped lead his team to back-to-back victories. First, with Hull 1–0 down against West Ham, he burst into the box and calmly fired in an equaliser.

Goooooooooooooooooooaaaaaaaaaaaaaaaalllllllllllllllll lllllllll!!!!!!!!!!!!!!!!!!!

'Let's gooooooooooo!' Andy cried out, swinging his left fist in the air.

Then in their next match against Middlesbrough, Hull fought back from 1–0 down again. Andy's cross looped up off a defender and caused chaos in the penalty area, until eventually Lazar Marković poked the ball in. Game on! Suddenly, the Tigers were flying forward on the attack at every opportunity.

Abel set up Oumar Niasse. 2–1!

Then Kamil Grosicki set up Abel. 3–1!

Middlesbrough scored to make it 3–2 just before half-time, but after the break, Andy secured the victory by whipping in a fantastic free kick for his friend Harry to head home. 4–2!

Hurray, Hull were out of the relegation zone! But sadly not for long. They soon slipped back down and after one last devastating 4–0 defeat at Crystal Palace, it was official. Hull had been relegated from the Premier League.

Noooooo, not that horrible sinking feeling again! As he trudged off the pitch, Andy felt the same disappointment and despair as he had two years earlier. He had tried so hard to help turn things around, but in the end, he had failed.

So, what next – a return to the Championship? No, as much as Andy loved Hull, it felt like the right time to move on and stay up in the Premier League. Surely, by now he had proved that was where he belonged? Hopefully, Burnley would be back during the summer to try and sign him again, and maybe so would some other, even bigger teams too...

CHAPTER 14

LIVERPOOL? LET'S GO!

In the summer of 2017, Jürgen Klopp had just
completed his second season as Liverpool manager,
and overall, it had been a successful one. New
signings Joël Matip, Gini Wijnaldum and Sadio Mané
had helped strengthen the squad and The Reds had
finished fourth in the Premier League, securing a
return to the Champions League.

But while Klopp was pleased, he was never
satisfied. He knew that there were still areas to
improve in his team, and the left-back role was top of
his list. Young Spaniard Alberto Moreno looked good
going forward but dodgy in defence, so for most of the

2016–17 season, Klopp had played James Milner in that position instead, even though he was right-footed and really a midfielder.

That couldn't carry on, but who should Liverpool sign? With his team's fast-paced, pressing style of play, Klopp wanted a left-back who was young, energetic, and loved to attack. Leicester City's Ben Chilwell was the top name on the list, but when Liverpool made a £7-million bid, it was rejected straight away.

'We want at least £10-million,' Leicester told them.

Liverpool didn't want to pay that much, though, so they moved on to their next target: a Scottish left-back who had just been relegated with Hull…

Andy! Yes, he definitely fitted the description:

Young? Tick!

Energetic? Tick!

Loves to attack? Tick!

Plus, there were two other things that really impressed the Liverpool scouts about Andy: his hard work and his positive attitude. 'Mentality monsters' – that's what the club's Sporting Director, Michael 'Eddie' Edwards, and Director of Research, Dr Ian

Graham, were looking for when it came to new signings. They wanted players with a will to win, who would fight to the final whistle and never give up.

That was Andy! He had shown his fearlessness, as well as his football skills, during Hull's 2–0 win against Liverpool the previous season. Not only had he defended well against Mané that day, but he had also pushed forward and delivered lots of dangerous crosses into the box.

Klopp was impressed by Andy's performance, and by his backstory too. Wow, any player who had made it all the way from the Scottish Third Division to the English Premier League had to have serious mental strength!

When Andy first heard that Liverpool were interested in signing him, he was buzzing with excitement, and one meeting with Klopp later, his mind was made up. The Liverpool manager was looking to challenge for all the major trophies, and Andy was desperate to be a part of such an ambitious project. The chance to play for a top club in the Champions League and challenge for the Premier

League title? It was a no-brainer – great, let's go!

Unfortunately, however, switching clubs wasn't quite that quick and easy. Hull didn't really want to let Andy leave, and so it took a long time to get the deal done. It was only in late July, during Hull's pre-season training camp in Portugal, that Andy finally got the news he'd been waiting weeks for:

'You're signing for Liverpool!'

Hurray! For a fee of £8-million, Andy officially became a Red, following in the footsteps of his dad's great Scottish hero, Kenny Dalglish. And when Andy and his family first arrived at Anfield for a tour of the stadium, who was there waiting to greet them in the car park? Yes, King Kenny himself! Andy couldn't believe it, and neither could his dad, who just stood there lost for words in front of his idol. Luckily, Kenny spoke instead:

'Welcome to Liverpool!'

Andy was really looking forward to getting started and fighting for the left-back spot. From his days at Hull, he knew how good his new teammates were: Sadio, Gini, James, Roberto Firmino, Philippe

Coutinho, Jordan Henderson... Wow, he was really going to have to up his game to reach their level! Unfortunately, Andy had missed his new club's pre-season tour to Hong Kong, but hopefully if he worked hard enough in training, he would get a chance to play eventually...

For Liverpool's first Premier League match of the season, Alberto started at left-back and Andy wasn't even on the subs bench. After drawing 3–3 with Watford, however, Klopp decided to make some changes in defence for their next game against Crystal Palace:

At right back, Trent Alexander-Arnold was replaced by Joe Gomez,

At centre back, Dejan Lovren was replaced by Ragnar Klavan,

And at left-back, Alberto was replaced by... Andy!

Hurray, this was it: the day he had been waiting for. Andy was about to make his official Liverpool debut at Anfield, in front of over 53,000 fans! He was determined to take his chance to shine, just like he had at Queen's Park, Dundee United and Hull City.

Andy stood there in the tunnel, below the famous 'This is Anfield' sign, waiting to go out for the warm-up. His manager walked over and put an arm around his shoulder.

'Ready?' Klopp asked with a reassuring smile. 'Enjoy today – good luck, you're going to be great!'

Thanks, Boss! After that little confidence boost, Andy jogged out onto the pitch with an even greater will to win. He couldn't wait for kick-off. When it finally arrived, the atmosphere inside the stadium sounded even louder than he remembered. And there was that familiar song from his days at Celtic Park:

Walk on, walk on,
With hope in your heart,
And you'll never walk alone,
YOU'LL NEVER WALK ALONE!

As he listened, Andy took a moment to think about how far he had come over the last few years, from Annan Athletic's Galabank Stadium all the way to Anfield. Then, with a jump and a last shake of his legs, he focused his mind on the football match ahead.

'Come on, Robbo!' his captain, Jordan, clapped and cheered over the noise.

Klopp wanted his full-backs to get forward as much as possible, and so that's exactly what Andy did. Early on, he raced up the left wing and delivered a dangerous cross into the box that almost reached Gini.

'Unlucky, great ball!' his manager shouted from the sidelines.

Andy was off to a strong start at Anfield, and he carried on creating chances all game long.

PING! He whipped in another curling cross for Joël to attack, but he somehow headed wide.

PING! He picked out Sadio in the middle, but he scuffed his shot.

PING! He slid the ball across the six-yard box, but the Palace keeper dived down and stopped it.

Oh dear, was Andy's debut going to end in a disappointing 0–0 draw? No, at last, Liverpool scored, and he played a key part in the goal. From wide on the left, Sadio passed the ball inside to Andy, who played it back for the one-two. Then, after a bit of a

scramble in the box, Sadio fired a shot past the keeper.
1–0!

'Come onnnnnnn!' Andy cried out joyfully, running
over to join in with the team celebrations.

Twenty minutes later, when the final whistle blew,
he had completed the dream debut for any defender:

A cleansheet,

A win,

And most amazing of all,

The man of the match award.

The huge smile didn't leave Andy's face for hours.
What a way to kick off his new life at Liverpool!

CHAPTER 15

LEARNING LESSONS (AT LIVERPOOL)

After getting off to such a flying start, surely Andy deserved to stay in the Liverpool starting line-up? But no, for their next Premier League match, he wasn't in the matchday squad at all. Alberto played instead against Arsenal, and against Manchester City too.

Why? What had he done wrong? When Andy asked his manager, Klopp was happy to explain: 'Robbo, you're quick, a good footballer, a good crosser, but you have to improve your defensive skills.'

Okay, Boss – no problem! Work on his weaknesses? Yes, Andy could definitely do that – plus he was still adapting to Liverpool's different style of football. At

Hull, he was used to defending deep and sticking tightly to the winger he was marking, whereas Klopp preferred his team to press higher up the pitch and focus on defending areas rather than individual opponents. It was a totally new system to learn, but Andy was determined to master it as quickly as possible.

A few weeks later, he was back in Klopp's starting line-up for their home match against Burnley. Hurray, all that hard work was paying off! Everything went well until the twenty-seventh minute, when a cross came into the Liverpool box. It flew past the centre-backs and landed at the back post, where Scott Arfield beat Andy to the bouncing ball and scored.

Nooooooooooo! The goal certainly wasn't all his fault and the Reds did fight back and equalise, but Andy didn't play again in the Premier League for two whole months. Why? Because he still needed to work on his defensive skills.

That wasn't his only problem, though. When he went back to see his manager again and ask what he could do to improve, Klopp gave him another honest answer: 'You look lost because you have no confidence.'

Although it wasn't a nice thing to hear, Andy knew that his manager was right. He didn't just need to get better at defending; he also needed to start believing in himself a lot more. Where had the old fearless Andy gone, with the never-give-up attitude? He had earned the right to become a Liverpool player but now he had to prove that he truly belonged at such a big club.

Okay, Boss – no problem! Inspired by his manager's words and experienced teammates like James and Jordan, Andy came back fighting. He attacked each training session with energy and positivity again, as if to say 'Boss, pick me!'

Sadly, that didn't happen straight away, though. Andy didn't come on against Huddersfield Town or Chelsea, and he wasn't even on the bench against West Ham, or Southampton, or Stoke City...

'Just be patient – you'll get another opportunity!' his friends and family kept telling him, but Andy absolutely hated watching his team from the stands. At his old clubs, he had played almost every single match, so it felt horrible and wrong to not be out there on the pitch. Those difficult weeks did, however, make him even more determined to take his next chance when it finally came.

Andy's moment arrived in early December, when unfortunately Alberto injured his ankle badly in a match against Spartak Moscow. Oh no! Watching his teammate limp off the pitch in tears, Andy felt so sorry for him, but at the same time, he couldn't help thinking what it might mean for his own Liverpool career. Because who would Klopp pick to take Alberto's place?

That night in the Champions League, the answer was James, but a few days later in the Premier League, it was... Andy! Right, this was it: his time to shine and show his manager how much he'd improved.

Let's gooooooooooooo!

In the Merseyside Derby against Everton, Andy did everything that Klopp asked him to do and more.

He defended well when he needed to, and he flew forward on the attack as often as possible.

He battled fearlessly for every ball, and his energy

seemed endless.

The only thing missing was the killer final ball. For once, all of Andy's crosses were cleared away, and his one shot flew high over the bar. Oh well, all he needed was more match practice...

Away at Bournemouth, Andy led Liverpool forward on a quick attack. After passing the ball through to Philippe, he continued his run up the wing, but the little Brazilian didn't need him. Instead, he danced his way into the box and scored. 1–0!

'Yesssssssss!' Andy cheered, throwing his arms up in the air.

At last, after a difficult beginning, he was really starting to feel like he belonged in the Liverpool team now. During the busy Christmas period, he played in all three matches, and then, after a game-off on New Year's Day, he was back in the team for the big one against the Premier League leaders, Manchester City.

Andy couldn't wait, and neither could his teammates. Although they were eighteen points behind City in the table, this was their chance to send out a warning for next season. 'Get ready – we're going to challenge you for the title!'

At half-time, the score was 1–1, but in the second half, Liverpool stormed ahead with three goals in eight minutes.

First Roberto scored with a cheeky chip over the keeper. 2–1!

Then Sadio slammed an unstoppable shot into the top corner. 3–1!

And finally, Mohamed Salah intercepted a pass from Ederson and curled a shot into the empty net. 4–1!

Woah, what was going on? Liverpool were winning 4–1! City did pull two goals back in the last ten minutes, but the Reds managed to hold on for a famous victory.

'Hurrraaaaayyyyyyyyyyy!' the Anfield crowd cheered wildly at the final whistle.

What a win! But for all the brilliant goals their team had scored, most Liverpool fans' favourite moment of the match involved a bit of defending by their left-back. In the seventy-fourth minute, after successfully marking Raheem Sterling out of the game, Andy sprinted forward from his own half to press Bernardo Silva.

'Go on!' the fans urged.

So when Bernardo then passed the ball back to Kyle Walker, Andy didn't give up. Instead, he kept going.

'Go on!'

Even when John Stones passed the ball all the way back to Ederson in goal, Andy kept going.

'Go on!'

His epic, seventy-yard run only ended when the referee awarded a free kick to City, but the Liverpool fans didn't care about that. They stood together to clap and sing for their fearless and tireless new hero:

'ANDY, ANDY, ANDY, ANDY ROBERTSON!'

CHAPTER 16

CHAMPIONS LEAGUE HIGHS AND LOWS

What a turnaround! Thanks to lots of hard work and a positive attitude, Andy had gone from sitting on the sidelines to become Liverpool's first choice left-back. And Klopp wasn't just picking him for Premier League matches anymore; he was also letting him play in the Champions League too.

The Champions League! As a kid, watching Celtic take on top teams like Juventus and Bayern Munich, Andy had always dreamed of starring in Europe's biggest club competition. Now here he was, walking out onto the pitch in Porto and lining up for the famous tournament anthem. As he listened, Andy felt the hairs on his neck stand up with a mix of pride and excitement. What a journey it had already been, from the Scottish Third Division all the way to the Champions League! And at the age of twenty-three, he was only really just getting started.

ZOOM! On his European debut, Andy raced up and down the left wing all game long, as Liverpool ran riot against Porto. By the end of the game, Sadio had scored a hat-trick and they had won 5–0. Last 16 tie over, on to the quarter-finals!

There, they faced their English rivals, Manchester City. It was going to be a really tough battle, but Andy was feeling confident about his team's chances. Liverpool had beaten City last time in the Premier League, and since then, they had made their defence even better by signing Dutchman Virgil van Dijk. In the past, Andy had played against Virgil, for Dundee United vs Celtic, but he much preferred being on the same team as him! He was quick, he was strong, and best of all, he was a real leader at the back. Virgil was so calm and composed on the pitch that he made everyone around him feel more confident.

So, yes, Liverpool could definitely knock City out

of the Champions League! In the first leg at Anfield, the Reds raced into a 3–0 lead after only thirty-one minutes thanks to goals from Mohamed, Alex Oxlade-Chamberlain and then Sadio.

Hurrrraaaaaaaaaaaaaayyyyy!

With Anfield rocking and roaring all around him, Andy stood there enjoying the moment and the greatest atmosphere he had ever experienced.

It wasn't game over yet, though. In the second half, Andy swapped his flying forward runs for determined defending. With his speed and energy, he managed to keep Sterling quiet once again, and so at the final whistle, Liverpool had a clean sheet to go with their win. What a night!

It wasn't the time for big celebrations, however, because they still had the second leg to play, away at the Etihad Stadium. Could Liverpool hold on and make it through to the semi-finals?

When City scored a goal in the second minute, suddenly the Liverpool fans grew nervous, but their heroes on the pitch never stopped believing. They stayed strong, fought hard for every ball, and then as City pushed more and more players forward, Mohamed and Roberto pounced on two mistakes. Now, it really was game over – Liverpool were winning 2–1 on the night, and 5–1 in total!

'Come onnnnnn!' Andy cried out when the final whistle blew, and then he rushed over to celebrate with James and Trent. What a victory and what a team! He felt so proud to be a part of it. Could Liverpool now go all the way to Champions League glory?

'Yes, we can!' the players cheered together with confidence.

It certainly looked that way in the semi-final against Mohamed's old club Roma, when Liverpool went 5–0 up at Anfield. But after conceding two late goals, they then almost threw it all away in the second leg in Italy: 7–3, 7–4, 7–5… But fortunately, with Liverpool still hanging on to a 7–6 lead, Roma ran out of time to score again.

'Yesssssssssss!' Andy roared with joy and relief as he ran over to James, who was lying flat on the grass in disbelief. 'Milly, we did it!'

Later that night, once the incredible news had properly sunk in, Andy posted a message to his fans on social media: 'WHAT A FEELING!! Champions league final!!'

The last club standing in Liverpool's way were the thirteen-time European Champions, Real Madrid. Their team was full of superstars, from Sergio Ramos at the back to Cristiano Ronaldo and Karim Benzema in attack. Although Liverpool didn't have as much experience in their side, they had lots of talent and lots of belief. If they worked hard and performed at their best in the biggest game of their lives, then why couldn't they lift that Champions League trophy?

'Come on, let's goooooo!' Jordan called out as he led the team out onto the pitch in Kyiv.

As he took his position at left-back, Andy tried not to think about all the emotional messages he'd received from family and friends, and the fact that he was about to play in a Champions League final. The game didn't really feel any different to other important ones in the past, like the Scottish Cup Final with

Dundee United, or the Championship Play-off Final with Hull City. It was just another football match that he was desperate to win.

For the first twenty-five minutes, the match was tense and end-to-end, with chances for both teams. After that, however, the luck went against Liverpool. First, Mohamed limped off with a shoulder injury, and then early in the second half, Real Madrid scored one of the strangest goals that Andy had ever seen.

It all started when the Liverpool goalkeeper, Loris Karius, rushed out to the edge of his penalty area to make an easy catch. Right, who should he throw it to now? He had Andy to his left, calling for the ball, but instead, he tried to roll it right to Dejan. The problem was that Benzema had guessed what he was going to do, and he stuck out his leg and deflected it into the net. 1–0!

Noooooooooooo, what a disaster! Liverpool weren't losing for long, though. Four minutes later, Dejan headed the ball goalwards and Sadio poked it past the keeper. 1–1! Yesssssssssssssssss, they were back in the game!

There was heartbreak to come, however. Marcelo crossed from the left and Real Madrid's substitute, Gareth Bale, jumped up and scored a breathtaking bicycle kick. 2–1!

After watching the ball land in the Liverpool net, Andy turned away in despair. How on earth had he scored that? There was nothing they could do to stop a wondergoal like that.

'Come on, keep going!' Klopp urged his team on from the touchline.

However, as Liverpool attacked, searching for another equaliser, disaster struck for a third time. Andy didn't think there was much danger as Bale went for a long-distance strike, but his swerving shot slipped straight through Karius's gloves. 3–1!

NOOOOOOOOOOOOO! Andy held his head in his hands. It was all over now for Liverpool. They had lost the Champions League final.

On the long journey home, however, it wasn't all doom and gloom. Yes, it was a painful, disappointing defeat, but the Liverpool players really believed that it was just the start of their journey, not the end. They had taken a huge step forward by reaching the Champions League final, and now they had to learn from the experience, and carry on improving together.

Andy couldn't wait. Over the last six months of the 2017–18 season, he had really proved himself as a Liverpool player, and so he was feeling very positive about the future. 'Thank you for your amazing support this campaign,' he told his fans, 'we will be back stronger next season!!'

CHAPTER 17

NEW SCOTLAND SKIPPER (IN THE UEFA NATIONS LEAGUE)

That summer, most of Liverpool's stars travelled to Russia to compete in the 2018 World Cup, but sadly Andy was not among them. Scotland had failed to qualify, for what was now the tenth major international tournament in a row.

No, not again!

Although there had been some good moments – a 2–2 draw with England, Andy's lovely goal against Lithuania – ultimately, Scotland had finished third in their group behind England and Slovakia. That simply wasn't good enough. It was time to make some changes. So first Scotland appointed a new manager, Alex McLeish, who in September 2018 appointed a new captain. For years, midfielder Scott Brown had worn the armband, but now the national team would be led by... Andy!

Wow, Scotland skipper – it was the new proudest achievement of his football career! He just wished his Auntie Vera had still been alive to see him wear the armband.

'It's a massive honour for me and my family,' Andy told the media, before making his ambitions clear. 'I look forward to trying to lead this country back to major tournaments.'

Andy's first game as Scotland captain ended in a 4–0 defeat to Belgium, but three days later, he led his team out again, in the UEFA Nations League against Albania. The new tournament was a great opportunity for Scotland because the winners of each group would earn an automatic place in the play-offs for Euro 2020. 'Come on, let's do this!' Andy cried out with passion, while the players walked out of the tunnel and onto the pitch at Hampden Park.

At half-time, the score was still 0–0, but early in the second half, Scotland played their way up the left wing. Andy swapped passes with Kieran Tierney, who fed the ball forward to Stuart Armstrong, who laid it back for Andy...

PING! His high curling cross dropped for Steven Naismith at the back post. 1–0!

Yessssssssssss! Andy punched the air as the Tartan Army went wild up in the stands. Twenty minutes later, Steven scored a second goal to seal the victory. Hurray, an exciting new era had begun!

Or had it? Scotland's next result was a really disappointing 2–1 defeat to Israel, but they bounced back brilliantly away in Albania.

Winger Ryan Fraser cut inside and curled a shot into the bottom corner. 1–0!

Steven Fletcher scored from the penalty shot. 2–0!

After winning the ball back and racing up the left wing, Andy played it across to Ryan Christie, who slid a perfect pass through to James Forrest. 3–0!

'Get in – great work, lads!' Andy cheered happily as he high-fived his teammates.

To top their group, Scotland now just needed to beat Israel at home, and their captain was full of

belief that they could do it. 'Hopefully we'll take
the confidence from Albania into this match,' Andy
said. 'We want everyone to get behind us, give us
good backing, and hopefully we can put in a similar
performance to the one in Albania.'

But despite the Tartan Army's support at Hampden
Park, Scotland found themselves 1–0 down after ten
minutes. Uh-oh, was yet another tournament about to
end in failure? No, Andy wasn't giving up, and neither
were the other Scottish players. They were going to
keep fighting until the final whistle.

'Come on, we've got plenty of time to turn this
around!'

And that's exactly what they did.

In the thirty-fourth minute, Stuart's shot was
blocked, but the rebound fell to James. 1–1!

Just before half-time, Andy played a long ball
forward to Steven Fletcher, who flicked it on to Ryan
Christie, who set up James to score again. 2–1!

Then midway through the second half, Andy poked
a pass through to Ryan Fraser, who crossed the ball
into the box for James to complete his hat-trick. 3–1!

'Yessssssssssss!' Andy cried out from the middle of the big team hug. What an incredible comeback!

That wasn't the end of it, though. Things did get a bit nerve-wracking when Israel scored again with twenty minutes to go, but Scotland worked hard and worked together to hold on for a massive win.

'Well done, boys – we did it!' Andy screamed with delight. He was one step closer to achieving his aim of leading his country back to a major tournament. Hopefully, Scotland would qualify for Euro 2020 the easy way, by topping their group, but if not, at least now they had a play-off spot secured.

CHAPTER 18

BATTLE OF THE LIVERPOOL FULL-BACKS!

What a big, breakthrough year it had been for Andy. As well as becoming the Scotland skipper, he had also gone from Liverpool zero to Liverpool hero. He didn't just sit back feeling satisfied with his work, though; no, he was always looking for ways to take the next step forward. Now that his confidence was up and his defending had improved, he was ready to do more of what he did best for his club: attack!

Klopp wanted his full-backs to be defenders when Liverpool didn't have the ball, and then wingers once they won it back.

'Don't worry, a midfielder will cover you if you race forward,' the manager explained.

Yes, Boss! It was like Andy's old days at Dundee United all over again. The system suited players like him and Trent perfectly, because they were two of the best crossers in the Premier League. Plus, they were young, fit, and improving all the time.

'I bet I get more assists than you this season,' Trent announced at the start of the 2018–19 campaign. It was always good to create a bit of friendly competition.

'You're on,' Andy replied straight away with a smile. 'Let the battle begin!'

After twenty minutes of their opening game against West Ham, Liverpool were winning 1–0, and so was Andy. ZOOM! he raced up the left and into the box, then PING! he slid the ball across to Mohamed for an easy tap-in at the back post.

'Thanks, Robbo!' Mohamed cheered, giving his left-back a big hug.

And that was just the beginning for Andy. A few weeks later away at Leicester City, he weaved his way up the wing again, this time setting up Sadio to score. 1–0!

'Come onnnnnnn!' Andy roared with passion. He was one of Liverpool's key players now, and with four wins out of four, they were off to the perfect start in the Premier League. The big question now was: could they keep it up?

'Yes, we can!' the Reds replied. With a 5–1 thrashing of Arsenal, Liverpool finished 2018 seven points clear at the top of the table. 'At last, we're going to win the league again!' the fans began to dream. Was their twenty-nine-year wait about to end?

Four days later, however, Liverpool lost 2–1 to rivals Manchester City, despite another brilliant assist from Andy. And when the Reds then drew with Leicester and West Ham, their lead at the top got smaller and smaller. Suddenly, the title race was on, but so was the battle of Liverpool's flying full-backs.

Andy set up the winning goal for Sadio in a 4–3 thriller against Crystal Palace. Andy 5 Trent 3! Liverpool's left-back curled a beautiful pass into Gini's path as they beat Bournemouth 3–0. Andy 6 Trent 3!

Andy got two assists and Trent got three in a 5–0 win against Watford. Andy 8 Trent 6!

'Watch out, I'm coming for you!' Trent joked at the final whistle.

Liverpool were in fantastic form, but unfortunately for them, so were Manchester City. With eight games to go, City were one point ahead at the top of the Premier League table.

'All we can do is win every last game,' Klopp told his players, 'and hope that City slip up.'

The Liverpool team listened to their manager and followed his instructions: eight games, eight victories. And for Andy, three more important assists:

WHIP! He curled in an incredible cross for Roberto to head home in their big game against Tottenham. 1–0!

PING! PING! He picked out Sadio and then Mohamed with two more inch-perfect crosses against Huddersfield. 3–0... 5–0!

'Andy Robertson delivers once again!' cried the commentator on TV.

Andy was up to an amazing eleven assists for the season now, and one game later, so was Trent. Oooooh – they were tied with one game to go!

'Mate, why do you have to be so competitive – can't you just let me win for once?' Andy joked.

That was just a battle going on in the background, though. Their full focus was on the fight for the Premier League title. There was still only one point separating the top two teams, so it all came down to the last day of the season.

Before kick-off, Klopp repeated the same old message: 'First, we need to beat Wolves, and then we can worry about whether City beat Brighton, okay?'

'Yes, Coach!'

There was a tense atmosphere at Anfield that day, but in the seventeenth minute, Sadio lifted the mood by giving Liverpool the lead. 1–0!

'Hurraaaaay!' A cheer went up around Anfield, followed ten minutes later by an even louder roar. Even the players out on the pitch could sense what had happened: Brighton were beating City! If things stayed the same, Liverpool would be crowned Champions...

'Come on, stay focused!' Jordan yelled out to his teammates. Their job wasn't done yet.

Yes, captain! Moments later, Andy raced forward and unleashed a ferocious strike, but the Wolves keeper stopped it with an excellent diving save. Awwwww – so close to his first goal of the season! At last, in the eighty-first minute, Liverpool did score again. With a quick look-up, Trent whipped one of his trademark crosses around the centre-backs and down onto Sadio's diving head. 2–0!

Oh, and in the battle of the full-backs: Trent 12 Andy 11!

Liverpool's heroes shared a smile and a hug, but by then, they knew that the title race was over. The buzz around Anfield had faded completely, a clear sign that City were now beating Brighton.

After the final whistle, as he walked around Anfield thanking the fans, Andy felt a strange mix of pride and pain. They had all worked so hard and played so well for thirty-eight games, but to lose the title by one stupid point was really tough to take. Liverpool did have one thing to help ease their Premier League disappointment, though...

'An incredible season but unfortunately we just fell

short!' Andy wrote on social media later that night. 'We now have to pick ourselves up and look forward to Madrid.'

Madrid? Yes, against all the odds, Liverpool had battled their way back to another Champions League Final.

CHAPTER 19

SECOND TIME LUCKY/ BOUNCING BACK: CHAMPIONS OF EUROPE!

Back-to-back Champions League finals – very few teams had ever achieved that, but the Liverpool players never stopped believing. First, they battled their way out of the 'Group of Death' against PSG and Napoli.

'Yesssssssss!' Andy yelled, swinging his left fist at the sky. Phew, they were going through!

Then, with their confidence up, Liverpool cruised through the next two rounds, beating Bayern Munich comfortably and thrashing Porto in the quarter-finals. It was so far so good on the road back to the Champions League final, but they were about to face their biggest challenge: Barcelona and Lionel Messi.

According to the teamsheet, the little Argentine magician was playing as a right winger, which meant it was Andy's job to mark him. But really, the world's greatest footballer had the freedom and the skill to roam all over the pitch.

Challenge accepted! In the twelfth minute away at the Nou Camp, Andy stopped Messi from scoring with a sensational sliding tackle, but in the end, it was a losing battle. First Luis Suárez put Barcelona ahead, and then Messi made sure of the win with a tap-in, followed by an unstoppable free kick.

After watching the ball fly into the top corner, Andy turned away in defeat. Nooooooooooo! Despite a decent performance, Liverpool had somehow lost the first leg 3–0.

So, was it game over already? No, Andy and his teammates weren't giving up without the greatest fight of their lives. Back home at Anfield, anything was possible! There, they believed they could beat anyone 4–0:

Even Barcelona,

And even without Mohamed and Roberto, who

were both out injured.

Liverpool, Liverpool!

With the home crowd behind them, it only took Liverpool six minutes to score their first goal. Jordan's shot was saved, but Divock Origi scored the rebound. 3–1!

'Come on, we can do this!' Andy cried out with conviction as the team raced back for the restart.

The Reds were on their way, but as well as scoring three more goals, they would also have to keep Messi quiet. That wouldn't be easy, but Andy soon found a way to unsettle him. When the Barcelona forward fell to the ground after a tackle from Fabinho, Liverpool's left-back gave him a cheeky shove in the back of his head to say, 'Welcome to Anfield'.

'Hey!' Messi complained, but the referee waved play on. Mission completed!

At half-time, however, Andy's match came to an early end. He had tried his best to carry on after a nasty kick from Suárez, but the pain in his leg was getting worse and worse.

'Sorry Robbo – you're coming off,' Klopp decided in

the dressing room. 'Gini, you're coming on.'

Although Andy was really disappointed, it turned out to be one of the best substitutions that Liverpool had ever made.

While Andy was in the physio room, Trent whipped a low cross into the box, where Gini timed his run to perfection. BANG! – 3–2!

And then, while Andy was in the shower, Gini scored again. 3–3!

When Andy heard the score, he couldn't believe it. Wow, Liverpool had done it – they were level! One more goal – that's all they needed now to pull off one of the greatest fightbacks in football history. Andy got dressed in a hurry and hobbled out to the bench to cheer his teammates on for the last twenty minutes.

Come on, lads – you can do this!

The atmosphere inside Anfield was unbelievable. Could Liverpool now go on and win the match before it went to extra-time, while the Barcelona players were still in shock? With fifteen minutes to go, Trent raced up the wing again to win a corner-kick for Liverpool. He was about to walk away and let Xherdan Shaqiri take it, when he suddenly spotted Divock in space in the middle. TING! Trent had an amazing idea. If he took it really quickly, maybe they could catch Barcelona out... BANG! He whipped the ball into the box and Divock smashed it into the top corner. 4–3!

Liverpool's incredible comeback was complete! Andy was desperate to celebrate the goal with all of his teammates over by the corner flag, but he decided to wait until the final whistle blew. Then, he limped onto the pitch as quickly as his injured leg would let him.

'We're going to Madrid!' Andy cried out again and again, hugging each Liverpool player and coach that came past. Would he be fit enough to play in the biggest game of all, though? Of course he would – nothing was going to stop him.

After 'The Miracle of Anfield', Liverpool were feeling quietly confident about their second Champions League final in a row. If they could beat Messi's Barcelona 4–0, then surely, they could beat anyone!

Ahead of kick-off, the signs were good. Andy, Mohamed and Roberto were all back from injury and they were taking on a team that they knew very well – their English rivals, Tottenham. In the Premier League that season, Liverpool had beaten them twice, 2–1 on both occasions. They also had one other important advantage over their opponents: big game experience. Andy and his teammates already knew what playing in a Champions League final was like. This time, they knew what to do and were fully prepared to win it.

'Let's do this!' Jordan shouted, as he led the Liverpool team out into the tunnel.

Walking out onto the pitch, Andy kept looking forward, ignoring the glistening Champions League trophy to his left. That could wait; they needed to win the match first.

After that awful night in Kiev against Real Madrid, Andy had been sure that Liverpool would make it back to the final again. But to do it the very next year? It was almost too good to be true. So, would Liverpool

be second time lucky? Yes, and they were 1–0 up
before Andy had even had a touch!

Within seconds of kick-off, Jordan chipped a ball
over the top for Sadio to chase. With his speed, Sadio
got to it first and as he tried to cross it into the box,
the ball struck Moussa Sissoko on the arm.

'Handball!' Andy cried out, raising his left arm high
into the air.

The referee pointed to the spot straight away, and
after a check with VAR, the penalty was confirmed.
Up stepped Mo, who beat the keeper with ease. 1–0!

What a start! But while he celebrated the goal with
his teammates, Andy wasn't getting carried away just
yet. There was plenty of work still to do.

Having taken the lead, Liverpool didn't just sit deep
and defend. No, that wasn't their style at all. Instead,
they pushed forward looking for another goal, led by
their flying full-backs. First Trent hit a swerving strike
that flew just wide of the post, and then as half-time
approached, it was Andy's turn. Collecting the ball
deep in his own half, he raced his way up the left

wing until he reached the edge of the Tottenham box. Then BANG! he unleashed a powerful shot that Hugo Lloris had to tip over the bar.

'Oooooooooohh!' Andy groaned, bouncing up and down with disappointment. What a chance to score a Champions League final goal!

For most of the second half, Andy had to focus on the second part of his job – defending – but he still joined the Liverpool attack as often as he could.

WHIP! He curled in a teasing low cross that almost landed at Sadio's feet.

PING! He intercepted Lucas Moura's pass and quickly set Mohamed away on the counterattack.

'Keep going!' Klopp clapped and cheered on the sidelines.

Then, just when Liverpool were preparing themselves for a nervy last ten minutes, Divock scored to make it 2–0. Game over, final won!

'Yessssssss!' Andy screamed, jumping up on Divock's back in front of the Liverpool fans. They had done it; they were the new Champions of Europe!

After a few more minutes of focus, it was all over.
Andy sank to his knees, with his head in his hands,
overwhelmed with emotion. He was a European
Champion now!

'We did it, Robbo!' James cheered as he rushed over
to give him a big hug.

Yes, they had, and the feeling was so amazing that
Andy didn't have the words to describe it. Instead, he
moved around the pitch in a daze of disbelief, dancing
and singing with his teammates.

Liverpool! Liverpool! Liverpool!

It was party time for the players and supporters,
and soon, it was trophy time too. With his winner's
medal around his neck, Andy turned to his manager.
'This one's a lot better than last year!' he said with a
smile. Then he stood with his teammates on the stage,
waiting for Jordan to do his captain's job.

Ohhhhhhhhhhhhhhhhhhhhhhhhh…

Hurraaaaaaaaaaaaaaaaaaaaaaay!

Andy threw his arms high into the air, while flames
shot up all around them. What a feeling, what a night!

The comeback against Barcelona had been brilliant, but this was even better.

Campeones, Campeones, Olé! Olé! Olé!

'Just a wee guy from Glasgow living the absolute dream,' Andy posted on social media, alongside a photo of him lifting the Champions League trophy.

After taking lots of happy photos with his best friends at Liverpool, it was time for Andy's family to join him on the pitch. His mum, dad and brother, his partner Rachel, and their young son Rocco – he couldn't have done it without their love, support and sacrifice. This win was for all of them, and Andy was so glad to have them all there in Madrid to share it with him.

Following a long night of celebrations in Madrid, the players returned to England, ready for an extra-special event: Liverpool's trophy bus tour. Nearly a million fans filled the city streets to greet their football heroes, waving club flags and singing club songs.

'Wow, this is BIG!' Andy kept thinking to himself. Their Champions League success meant so much to so many people.

A few days later, once their achievement had properly sunk on, Andy sent an emotional message to his friend and captain, Jordan. Having looked back at their amazing season together, Andy finished by looking forward:

'Now let's go and win that Premier League trophy next season.'

CHAPTER 20

PREMIER LEAGUE CHAMPIONS...AT LAST!

As the 2019–20 season kicked off, it was now thirty years since Liverpool had last been crowned Champions of England. Thirty years! That was way too long for such a world-famous football club. The previous year, they had finished second, only one painful point behind Manchester City; could they bounce back and lift the title this time?

After their Champions League triumph, Andy and his teammates were full of belief, and they started the new season on fire.

Liverpool 4 Norwich City 1,

Southampton 1 Liverpool 2,

Liverpool 3 Arsenal 1,

Burnley 0 Liverpool 3…

Four wins out of four, and Andy was still waiting for his first assist! That came a week later against Newcastle, as Liverpool fought back from 1–0 down to win yet again. With his first clever touch, Andy skipped away from Emil Krafth, and with his second, he slid the ball across to Sadio, who slammed a shot into the top corner. 1–1!

'Yesssssssssss!' Andy yelled, throwing his arms out wide. It felt so good to play an important role for his team, as they chased their Premier League dream.

After that confidence boost, the key assists kept coming for Andy:

PING! He set up Roberto to score the winner against Chelsea.

PING! He set up Adam Lallana to score a late equaliser against Manchester United.

With ten games played, Liverpool were already up to twenty-eight points, six ahead of Manchester City in second place. 'Yes, this is it – this is going to be our season!' the fans dared to dream again, and the players were determined to lift the Premier League title for them this time. To do that, however, they would have to keep working hard and working together, as one mean, match-winning machine.

A week later away at Aston Villa, Liverpool looked to be heading for their first defeat of the season, but no, the Reds refused to give up. In the eighty-seventh minute, Sadio raced up the right wing and chipped the ball towards the back post – and which of their big game players was there to head it in? No, not Mohamed, not Roberto, not Divock – Andy! He timed his leap to perfection and powered the ball past the keeper. 1–1!

Goooooooooooooooooooaaaaaaaaaaaaaaaallllllllllllllllllllllllllll!!!!!!!!!!!!!!!!!!!!

ANDY, ANDY, ANDY, ANDY ROBERTSON!!

What a time to score his first Premier League goal for two years, and his first-ever header in professional football! That wasn't the end of the story, though. 'Come onnnnnnnn!' Andy yelled, waving his arm to lead his teammates back for the restart. A draw was better than a defeat, but a win was what Liverpool really wanted. And they got it! With seconds to go,

Trent whipped in one last corner, and Sadio flicked the ball on into the far corner of the net. 2–1!

Wow, another fantastic fightback! Liverpool were certainly showing they had what it took to be crowned Premier League champions, but could they keep it up? It was time for their toughest test of the season so far: Manchester City.

In the days leading up to the big game, Andy tried his best to ignore all the media build-up and the talk of rivalry and revenge. This wasn't a title-decider yet; it was just another match that he was determined to win for his team.

In the fifth minute, Andy controlled the ball in his own penalty area and calmly played a pass down the line to Sadio, who sprinted forward on a quick counterattack. The City defence managed to clear his cross away, but only as far as Fabinho, who scored with a superstrike from twenty-five yards. What a start for Liverpool!

'Right, now stay focused!' Jordan shouted as the match kicked off again. Yes, they were winning, but at 1–0, it was far from over. What they needed was a second goal…

Spotting Andy in lots of space, Trent switched the play from right to left with a beautiful long pass. As he raced onto it, Andy looked up and saw Mohamed making a brilliant run in behind the City defence. After taking a touch to control it, WHIP! he curled the ball towards the penalty spot, where it bounced up perfectly for Mohamed to head it in. 2–0!

As Anfield erupted with excitement, Andy punched the air and then raced over to celebrate with his teammates. It was one of his new favourites assists because he knew how important it could be.

At the final whistle, Liverpool were the winners, and they moved nine points clear of Manchester City at the top of the Premier League table. That was a very big gap, but the Reds weren't thinking ahead to the title yet. They were just focused on winning each and every match they played:

Crystal Palace away,

Brighton at home,

Everton at home,

Bournemouth away,

Watford at home...

By the beginning of 2020, Liverpool were leading the Premier League by a whopping sixteen points, and they were also the new club champions of the world, after beating Flamengo in the FIFA Club World Cup final. Hurray, another major trophy lifted!

'Right, that's another for the cabinet,' Andy tweeted, 'now back to England for Prem business.'

Surely, there was no stopping Liverpool now? At Anfield, their big rivals Manchester United did their best to spoil the party, but Virgil and Mohamed got the goals to defeat them too. At the final whistle, the Kop End sang loud and proud:

You're Never Gonna Believe Us,
You're Never Gonna Believe Us,
You're Never Gonna Believe Us...
We're Gonna Win the League!

What a moment and what a feeling! Andy had goosebumps just listening to them. Finally, even their most nervous fans were starting to believe.

Not even a surprise defeat to Watford could dash Liverpool's title dreams. However, for a few months, it looked like COVID-19 might.

When the Premier League suddenly stopped in early March 2020, Liverpool were twenty-two points clear and just days away from becoming Champions. What if they couldn't carry on? What if the season was over? Noooo, that would be so cruel!

For three long months, the Liverpool players stayed at home, keeping fit and hoping that they would get the chance to finish things off. For Andy, lockdown was a nice chance to work on his charity, 'AR26', help out the local foodbanks, and spend more time with Rachel, Rocco, and his young daughter, Aria. However, it turned out that doing DIY and gardening really wasn't for him.

'Get me back out on that football pitch!' he groaned.

At last, there was good news – it was safe for the Premier League to restart in June! But the bad news was that there would be no supporters allowed in the stadiums. What, no fans?! What was the point of football without fans? It didn't feel right, but they had to carry on. Liverpool had a title to win and Andy was determined to give the people at home something to cheer about.

In their first game back, the Reds could only draw 0–0 with Everton in an empty Goodison Park, but still, every single point took them towards their target – the Premier League trophy. And three days later, Liverpool were back to their best as they thrashed Crystal Palace. Andy even grabbed his eighth assist of the season, setting up Fabinho for another long-range rocket. 3–0!

'Huge performance from us today,' Andy tweeted afterwards. 'One step closer.'

In fact, if City failed to beat Chelsea, then the title would be Liverpool's... and that's exactly what happened! The match finished Chelsea 2 Manchester City 1.

At Stamford Bridge, the Chelsea players high-fived

and bumped elbows, but that was nothing compared to the celebrations in the city of Liverpool. Their team had done it; after thirty years and a delay due to the pandemic, at last they had won the Premier League title!

'It's been a long wait REDS but you deserve this night,' Andy posted on social media the next day, alongside a photo of a Liverpool shirt. On the back, written in big letters, it read:

'CHAMPIONS 19–20.'

CHAPTER 21

GOING TO
THE EUROS!

When Liverpool's title-winning season eventually ended, Andy was able to enjoy some quality time off with his family. But before long, he was back to work on the football pitch. For his club, he had another Premier League title to try and win, and for his country, he had a major tournament to try and reach.

Sadly, Scotland's qualification campaign for the delayed Euro 2020 championships had not gone according to plan. Under new manager, Steve Clarke, they had failed to finish in the top two places in Group I, after heavy defeats against Belgium and Russia. There was still hope of going to the Euros, though, because they had secured that play-off spot through the UEFA Nations League.

Andy tried his best to rally the Tartan Army: 'Need the whole nation behind us for the big game in October.' That 'big game in October' was the play-off semi-final against Israel, which Scotland won, but only after a tense penalty shoot-out.

'Come onnnnnn!' Andy cried out as he jumped into the arms of their heroic goalkeeper, David Marshall. They were now just one game away from going to the Euros.

The last nation standing in their way was Serbia. Winning away in Belgrade wasn't going to be easy, but the Scotland team spirit was stronger than ever. The players believed that together they could do it – lead their country back to a major tournament.

Let's gooooooooooo!

John McGinn almost scored in the first half, and then early in the second half, it was Andy's turn to go close. Lyndon Dykes raced up the right wing, cut inside and played the ball across to the left for his captain. Andy sprinted into the box and hit his shot first time, but instead of keeping calm, he blazed it high over the bar. Arghhh, what a big chance wasted!

Luckily, two minutes later, Scotland took the lead. Callum McGregor passed the ball through to Ryan Christie, who spun and fired a low shot in off the post. 1–0! As Ryan slid across the grass on his knees, Andy was the first player to reach him, followed by the rest of his ecstatic teammates.

Scotland! Scotland!

For the next forty minutes, they defended bravely, but with seconds left in the match, Luka Jović equalised for Serbia.

'Noooooooooooo!' Andy groaned, with his hands on his hips and his head thrown back in disappointment. They had come so close to victory, but now they had an extra thirty minutes of football to prepare for, and then… penalties again!

On the halfway line, the Scotland players stood together to watch the shoot-out with arms around each other's shoulders.

'Yesssssssss!' Andy punched the air as Leigh Griffiths scored,

And then Callum,

And then Scott McTominay,

And then Oli McBurnie,

And then Kenny McLean.

Now it was all down to Serbia's fifth taker, Aleksandar Mitrović. If he scored, the shoot-out would go to sudden death. Andy really hoped that he wouldn't have to take a spot-kick, but if his country needed him to, then of course he would do it.

But no, Mitrović stepped up and... David dived down and saved it! It was all over, and Scotland were the winners!

'YESSSSSSSSSSSSSS!' Andy roared up at the sky as the players celebrated together. He had done it; he had led Scotland to their first major tournament for twenty-three years.

'The lads gave absolutely everything tonight, I could not be prouder of every single one of them!' he wrote on social media that night. 'Oh and......WE ARE GOING TO THE EUROS'.

As the tournament got closer, the excitement grew and grew. Scotland would even get to play two of their games at home at Hampden Park, against the

ROBERTSON

Czech Republic and Croatia. And the other team in
their group? England!

'Bring it on!' Andy joked with Jordan and Trent.

After a disappointing Premier League season where
Liverpool had only finished third, seventeen points
behind Manchester City, Andy couldn't wait to
captain his country at Euro 2020.

Against the Czech Republic, Scotland started the
game well.

PING! Andy raced up the left wing and delivered a
dangerous cross to Lyndon, who poked his shot just
wide.

BANG! Andy curled a shot towards the top corner,
but the keeper tipped it over the bar.

But despite lots of good chances, Scotland just
couldn't score, and in the end they were punished by
two goals from Patrik Schick.

'Gutted,' Andy posted after the game. 'Stay
positive.'

Next up: England at Wembley. Some people were
predicting a heavy defeat, but in fact, the match
finished 0–0 and Scotland could have won it. Stephen

O'Donnell had a powerful shot saved by Jordan Pickford and then Lyndon had a shot cleared off the line by Reece James. So close!

The result meant that to reach the Euro 2020 Round of 16, Scotland would now need to beat World Cup finalists, Croatia…

When Nikola Vlašić scored in the seventeenth minute, it looked like tournament over for Scotland, but no, the boys in navy blue came fighting back before half-time. Andy's cross was cleared as far as Callum, who fired the ball into the bottom corner. 1–1! Hurray, the dream was still alive!

In the second half, however, Croatia upped their game and showed their class. First Luka Modrić scored a stunner and then Ivan Perišić headed in a third to break Scottish hearts.

Noooooooo!

Although Andy was disappointed to be exiting Euro 2020 so soon, he was still proud of his team's performances. They had battled hard in a challenging group, and hopefully, this was just the beginning for them.

'We want to qualify for more tournaments and we want to make the people of this magnificent country even prouder!' Andy told the supporters. 'We will give everything we have to make this a reality. Scotland, it's been a pleasure.'

CHAPTER 22

UP FOR THE CUPS/BEATEN BY ONE POINT AGAIN

Goodbye Glasgow, hello Liverpool again! It was time for the Reds to get back to trophy-winning ways. Andy was heading into his fifth season at the club and to celebrate, he signed a big new five-year contract.

'Time flies when you're having fun!' he wrote on Twitter.

Other than Gini leaving for PSG, the Liverpool squad looked as strong as ever. Young centre-back Ibrahima Konaté was a superstar in the making, and having Virgil back from injury was like a brilliant, brand-new signing.

'Come on, let's do this!' Jordan cheered as the 2021–22 season kicked off. The Reds were ready to challenge for each and every trophy available, starting with:

1) The League Cup

Liverpool beat Leicester City in the quarter-finals, then Arsenal in the semi-finals, to set up a final against Chelsea. After 120 minutes of exciting, end-to-end football at Wembley, somehow the score was still 0–0. PENALTIES!

This time, the shoot-out did go to sudden death and Andy had to make the long walk forward for Liverpool. After placing the ball down carefully and taking a long, deep breath, he ran up and coolly sent Kepa the wrong way. 8–7 to Liverpool!

'Come onnnnnn!' Andy shouted up at their supporters above, urging them to make more noise.

Eventually, it all came down to the two keepers. Young Caoimhín Kelleher stayed calm and scored, but with the pressure on, Kepa blasted his penalty high over the bar.

'You hero!' Andy yelled out, rushing over to hug Caoimhín.

Liverpool trophy number one: lifted!

'YESSSSSSS!' Andy posted on social media with a picture of him cuddling the cup.

Right, onto the next one…

Klopp had Liverpool back to their unbeatable best, and by mid-May, the crazy quadruple was still on:

2) The FA Cup

Again, Liverpool made it all the way to the final, where again they faced Chelsea. And again, there were no goals and it went to penalties! The only difference was that this time, Andy was no longer on the pitch to take one. In sudden death, Alisson saved from Mason Mount, leaving Andy's left-back replacement, Konstantinos Tsimikas, to win it for Liverpool.

'We won! We won!' Andy screamed, as he sprinted from the subs bench to join in the celebrations.

For Liverpool, it was two trophies down, two to go…

3) The Premier League

After a frustrating first half of the season, Liverpool really found their best form in the second half. Suddenly, they were unstoppable again! With victory after victory, they cut down the gap between them and leaders Manchester City:

Eight points,

Then six,

Then three,

And then after a 2–0 win over Watford, just one!

'Nooooo, not this again!' Andy joked with Trent. The title race was looking like a repeat of 2018–19, but the Liverpool players were determined to fight until the very last whistle, especially their leader at left-back.

PING! Against Arsenal, Andy raced in to block Bukayo Saka's pass and then dribbled into the box, before setting up Roberto with his tenth league assist of the season. 2–0!

THUMP! In the Merseyside derby at Anfield, Andy ticked off another Liverpool dream. With a powerful header at the back post, he scored his first goal in front of the Kop. 1–0!

Goooooooooooooooooooaaaaaaaaaaaaaaaaallllllllllllllllll
lllllllll!!!!!!!!!!!!!!!!!!!!

'Hurrrraaaaaaaaaaaaaayyyyy!' Andy cheered, as he ran towards the corner flag, past Liverpool's loudest and most passionate fans. What a feeling!

BANG! Although Andy scored again on the last day of the season against Wolves, by then, it was sadly too little too late. Because although they were winning 3–1, Man City had fought back from 2–0 down to lead Aston Villa 3–2! So, Liverpool had lost the Premier League title by just one point again.

To deal with the disappointment, Andy tried to focus on the positives. 'Wasn't meant to be yesterday but so proud to be a part of this team!' he told his followers on Twitter. '1 more to go…'

4) The Champions League

The Reds were through to their third European final in just five years: 2018, 2019, and now 2022! There was just something so special about Liverpool in the Champions League. The players believed they couldn't lose. After battling their way past Inter Milan, Benfica and Villarreal, they made it to the main event, where they met… Real Madrid again!

A lot had changed since Liverpool's defeat in 2018. While their team had grown stronger, the Spanish giants had lost some of their most experienced stars, like Sergio Ramos and Cristiano Ronaldo. So now, Liverpool were actually the favourites to win.

Not that Andy was getting carried away, though. When he walked out onto the pitch at the Stade de France in Paris, he treated it like any of the other important matches he'd played in, for Queen's Park, Dundee United, Hull City, and Scotland.

Liverpool started the game strongly, like they loved to do. Mohamed's shot was saved by Thibaut Courtois and then Sadio's strike hit the post. So close! But as the Reds pushed forward looking for a goal, Real punished them on the counterattack. With Andy a long way up the pitch, Federico Valverde had lots of time and space to bring the ball forward and then deliver a cross to Vinícius Jr at the back post. 1–0!

Liverpool tried their best to fight back, but they just

couldn't find a way past Courtois, who was having the game of his life. When the final whistle blew, Andy sat down on the pitch with a devastated look on his face. Argggh, how had they not scored? They'd had so many chances but they'd failed to take any of them.

Once a few days had passed, however, Andy was able to do what he'd done throughout his amazing football career: focus on the positives and move forward past the setbacks. The fearless Scot simply never gave up:

Not when his boyhood club Celtic released him, aged fifteen,

Not when he was playing amateur football for Queen's Park,

Not when he lost the Scottish Cup final with Dundee United,

Not when he twice experienced relegation from the Premier League with Hull City,

Not during his difficult early days at Liverpool.

And look at him now! He was a European Champion, an English Champion, a League Cup winner and an FA Cup winner. Not bad for a skinny little boy from Glasgow!

Again and again, Andy had shown that he was a fighter and a winner, as well as a legendary left-back. So, he was confident that there would be lots more top trophies to come.

ROBERTSON
HONOURS

Hull City
🏆 Football League Championship play-offs: 2016

Liverpool
🏆 UEFA Champions League: 2018–19
🏆 UEFA Super Cup League: 2019
🏆 FIFA Club World Cup: 2019
🏆 Premier League: 2019–20
🏆 League Cup: 2021–22
🏆 FA Cup: 2021–22
🏆 FA Community Shield: 2022

Individual
🏆 PFA Scotland Young Player of the Year: 2013–14
🏆 PFA Scotland Team of the Year: 2013–14
🏆 PFA Premier League Team of the Year: 2018–19, 2019–20
🏆 UEFA Team of the Year: 2019
🏆 UEFA Champions League Team of the Season: 2021–22

ROBERTSON

26 THE FACTS

NAME: Andrew Robertson

DATE OF BIRTH: 11 March 1994

PLACE OF BIRTH: Glasgow

NATIONALITY: Scottish

BEST FRIEND: James Milner

CURRENT CLUB: Liverpool

POSITION: Left Back

THE STATS

Height (cm):	178
Club appearances:	442
Club goals:	20
Club assists:	78
Club trophies:	8
International appearances:	60
International goals:	3
International trophies:	0
Ballon d'Ors:	0

★ ★ ★ **HERO RATING: 86** ★ ★ ★

GREATEST MOMENTS

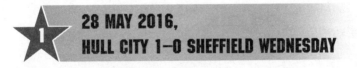

28 MAY 2016,
HULL CITY 1–0 SHEFFIELD WEDNESDAY

This was the happy day when Andy and his
teammates bounced straight back up to the Premier
League through the Championship play-offs. In front
of a huge crowd at Wembley, Hull were the team
on top and in the seventy-second minute, Mohamed
Diamé scored the winning goal. Hurraaaaay!

2
14 JANUARY 2018,
LIVERPOOL 4–3 MANCHESTER CITY

The Reds scored four goals in this victory over their
rivals, but most fans' favourite moment involved a bit
of defending by their left-back. In the seventy-fourth
minute, Andy sprinted forward, chasing the ball
from Silva, to Walker, to Stones, and then all the way
back to Ederson. 'ANDY, ANDY, ROBERTSON!' the
supporters sang for their tireless new hero.

3
1 JUNE 2019,
LIVERPOOL 2–0 TOTTENHAM

Back for his second Champions League final in two
years, this was the night when Andy became a
European Champion. Although he didn't score or set a
goal up, he played his part at both ends of the pitch. At
the final whistle, he sank to his knees with his head in
his hands, overwhelmed with emotion.

4 — 2 NOVEMBER 2019, ASTON VILLA 1–2 LIVERPOOL

The Reds were brilliant throughout their Premier League title-winning year, but this was a particularly big moment for Andy. With his team 1–0 down, he raced in at the back post, timed his leap to perfection and powered a header past the keeper. GOAL! From there, Liverpool fought back to win 2–1, and the rest is football history.

5 — 12 NOVEMBER 2020, SERBIA 1–1 SCOTLAND (WON ON PENALTIES!)

What a proud night for Andy and his national teammates! In their Euro 2020 play-off final, Scotland did everything right for eighty-nine minutes. They took the lead, they defended well, but then in the last minute, they conceded a late equaliser. Nooooooo! But don't worry, they won the penalty shoot-out. Hurray, Scotland were going to the Euros, their first major tournament for twenty-three years!

TEST YOUR KNOWLEDGE

QUESTIONS

1. Who was Andy's Celtic hero, and who was his dad's?

2. What two positions did Andy play before becoming a left-back?

3. Where was Andy when he got the call telling him to come in for Queen's Park pre-season?

4. Andy already knew all about manager Jackie McNamara before he signed for Dundee United, but why?

5. Andy signed for Hull City on the same day as which promising English defender?

6. When he first arrived at Liverpool, which other left-back was Andy competing with?

7. When Andy made his famous seventy-yard sprint, which club were Liverpool playing against?

8. Who did Andy replace as Scotland captain in 2018?

9. In the 2018–19 season, who won the battle of Liverpool's flying full-backs: Andy or Trent?

10. Andy led Scotland all the way to Euro 2020 – true or false?

11. How many Champions League finals has Andy appeared in?

1. Henrik Larsson and 'King Kenny' Dalglish. 2. Central midfield and left wing. 3. On an end-of-school holiday with his friends in Greece! 4. He had grown up watching him play full-back for Celtic. 5. Harry Maguire. 6. Alberto Moreno. 7. Manchester City. 8. Scott Brown. 9. Trent, by 12 assists to 11. 10. True – they qualified through the play-offs, beating Serbia on penalties. 11. Three – 2018, 2019 and 2022.

PLAY LIKE YOUR HEROES

RACE FORWARD AND CROSS
LIKE ANDY ROBERTSON

STEP 1: Warning: you're going to need lots of energy for this one! So before you get started, make sure you practise your 100m sprints.

STEP 2: When your team doesn't have the ball, stay in your position at left-back, and fight to win the ball back. But as soon as you do...

STEP 3: ZOOM! Race forward as fast as you can up the left wing, calling for the ball.

STEP 4: When it arrives, take a touch to control the ball and a second to look up and see where your teammates are in the box. Then...

STEP 5: WHIP! Curl the ball around the defenders and into the danger area, with plenty of power and loads of accuracy.

STEP 6: BANG!... GOAL! As your striker rushes towards the fans, race over to celebrate with them. You deserve to get at least some of the glory after your amazing assist.

CAN'T GET ENOUGH OF
ULTIMATE FOOTBALL HEROES?

**Check out heroesfootball.com
for quizzes, games, and competitions!**

**Plus join the Ultimate Football Heroes
Fan Club to score exclusive content
and be the first to hear about
new books and events.
heroesfootball.com/subscribe/**